Paddling the Waters of Vashon Island

Paddling the Waters of Vashon Island

A Circumnavigation and Some Adventures

by Biffle French

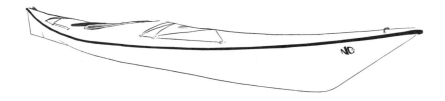

Paddling the Waters of Vashon Island
A CIRCUMNAVIGATION AND SOME ADVENTURES BY BIFFLE FRENCH

Lao Mei Publications
P.O. Box 13403
Burton, WA 98013 USA
www.LaoMeiPublications.com
info@LaoMeiPublications.com
Published 2008

PADDLING THE WATERS OF VASHON ISLAND Copyright © 2008 by Biffle French. All rights reserved. No part of this book may be reproduced or transmitted in any form by any means, electronic or mechanical, including photocopying, recording or by any information storage and retrieval system, without written permission from the author, except for the inclusion of brief quotations in a review.

Text, Maps, Illustrations and Cover Design by Biffle French
Author Photo by Wenwen Ma

Cover Photo Copyright © Ray Pfortner. Pfortner has been photographing nature and environmental issues professionally for over 30 years and Vashon-Maury Island for more than a decade. His photographs appear in books, magazines, and advertising campaigns internationally to promote public awareness of such issues. Pfortner maintains an extensive library of images. To see more of his work, visit www.RayPfortner.com.

"On Scientific Rigor", translated by Kenneth Krabbenhoft, "Fragments from an Apocryphal Gospel", translated by Stephen Kessler, from SELECTED POEMS by Jorge Luis Borges, edited by Alexander Coleman, copyright © 1999 by Maria Kodama. Used by permission of Viking Penguin, a division of Penguin Group (USA) Inc.

Illustration of Caprellid Amphipod © Eugene Kozloff. Reprinted by permission of the University of Washington Press from SEASHORE LIFE OF THE NORTHERN PACIFIC COAST by Eugene Kozloff

Publisher's Cataloging-in-Publication Data

French, Biffle.

    Paddling the waters of Vashon Island : a circumnavigation and some adventures / by Biffle French.

    p. cm.

    Includes bibliography.

    1. Northwest, Pacific—Description and Travel. 2. Sea Kayaking. 3. Boats and Boating—United States. I. Title

    797.1224

ISBN—978-0-9800636-0-8

Printed and bound in the United States of America.

Disclaimer

This book does not attempt to teach kayaking and it does not recommend kayaking in any way. The stories and information in this book are offered for entertainment only, and are not intended to be used for trip planning or any similar purposes.

Maps, tables and other data in this book are only sketches, and may be incorrect in any respect – they should never be used for navigation or trip planning. Official maps and information on geography as well as local weather and tide conditions are available from the U.S. Government or other sources, and information from those sources should always be used for trip planning in place of any information in this book.

Kayaking can be a dangerous sport and should only be attempted by trained, capable people with reliable equipment who have a good understanding of the local conditions that will occur at the day and time of their activity.

Be safe and paddle again tomorrow.

Acknowledgements

I want to thank the following people who generously gave me assistance and encouragement throughout this project: Wenwen Ma, my wife, for letting me follow my crazy dreams in spite of the obvious, Marjorie Biffle French, my mother, for her help in editing the manuscript, David Shull, University of Washington, friend and consultant on all things about the Puget Sound, Ray Pfortner for his beautiful cover photo, Rayna Holtz and Hester Kremer at the Vashon Library for helping with the difficult job of creating the CIP data.

Seek for the pleasure of seeking, not of finding...

Jorge Luis Borges

Table of Contents

Disclaimer	5
Acknowledgements	6
Preface	13

Prolog — 15
Spring Days — 16

Beginnings — 19
Beginning — 21
Becoming — 26
The Boat — 33

Paddles — 37
Paddles — 39
Rounding Point Dalco on the Flood — 40
Quartermaster Harbor — 51
Rounding Point Dalco on the Ebb — 59
Tragedy — 66
Point Robinson to Tahlequah — 69
Colvos — 77
Point Robinson to Portage — 89
Tahlequah to Gig Harbor — 95
Tramp Harbor to Dilworth Point — 101
Tango Charlie — 105
Vashon Ferry to Dilworth — 113
How Long is a Coastline? — 120

Nature — 123
Earth — 125
Air — 137
Fire — 141
Water — 143

Vashon — 155
Clearcut — 157
Blackberries — 159
Big Butts — 160
Fiestas — 167

Places — 171
Places — 173
Vashon Ferry Dock — 175
Tramp Harbor — 178
Point Defiance, Owen Beach — 181
Dockton — 185
Point Robinson — 188
Lisabeula — 190
Tahlequah — 192
Jensen Point — 195

Cold — 199
Cold Water Paddling — 201

Epilog — 205
Tomorrow — 207

Bibliography — 211

Table of Maps

Map 1 – Vashon and Vicinity   10
Map 2 – Rounding Point Dalco on the Flood 42
Map 3 – Quartermaster Harbor   52
Map 4 – Rounding Point Dalco on the Ebb 60
Map 5 – Point Robinson to Tahlequah   68
Map 6 – Colvos on Ebb Tide   76
Map 7 - Point Robinson to Portage   88
Map 8 – Tahlequah to Gig Harbor   94
Map 9 - Tramp Harbor to Dilworth Point 100
Map 10 - Tango Charlie   106
Map 11 - Vashon Ferry to Dilworth Point 114
Map 12 - North Vashon Places   174
Map 13 – South Vashon Places   182

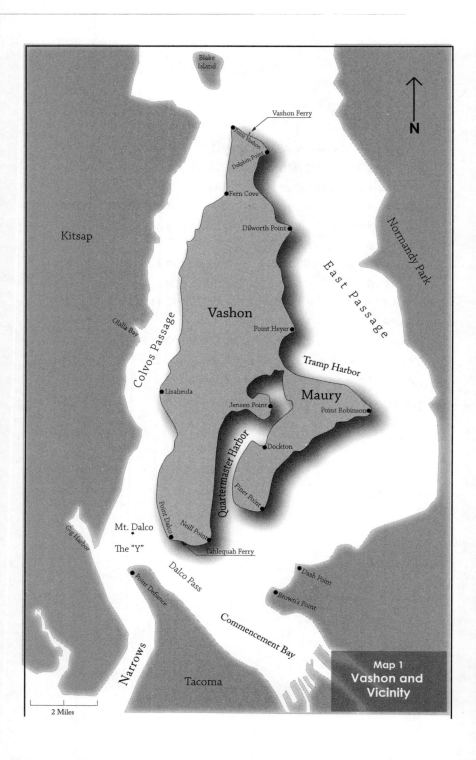

This little book is dedicated to kayakers everywhere and to the men and women who build their wonderful boats. May they paddle always and everywhere, forever.

About our Imprint:

Lao Mei Publications is a specialty publisher located on Vashon Island, WA. Lao Mei is Mandarin for "Gringo."

Preface

This is not the book I set out to write—at least I don't think so. The fact is that I can't really remember for sure. Our memories are not color movies of events, but unreliable little snips of sepia-tinted photos, stored away in a cupboard. The paddle I had today, its impression so fresh in my mind, is gone for good. The moment was delicious, but now that moment is past, leaving only a crumb, a little stump with a half-life measured in minutes—never years. The cormorant I saw zooming by close over the waves, the flying flags, the individual rollers, the extreme effort of moving the sluggish boat against the wind and over the waves, getting cold and wet, everything that made today's ride so special, are all indistinct now, and fading, never to be recovered.

The future is unrevealed, but sadly, so is the past. We think we can store our memories like so many hours of video. Later, we try to conjure the movie of our past, but the resolution is poor, and not one single shimmering pixel is reliable. Look at a Da Vinci painting, and concentrate on not moving your eye—you see just one spot clearly. Let your eye move and you form an impression, but it's only that. The closer you look, the more you see, but standing farther away gives you a view of something else entirely. So what matters, then? What's real?

What matters is the experience of the moment—that's the only thing that's real.

This is a book about moments, the best moments anyone could experience. I give them to you, such as they are, not as experiences, but as impressions. The experience is for you to seize later, as the moment presents itself to you. Because there *is* a movie to see, but it's *your* movie, not mine.

What I offer you here is a sketch of the things I saw, or rather a preview of what you will see if you just go where I went and do what I did.

Happy paddling!

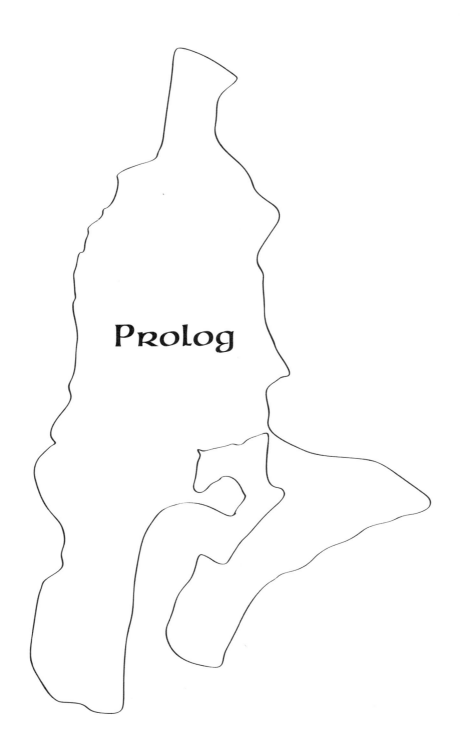

Prolog

Spring Days

Today is a beautiful, warm day in May. Rainier has a deep snow cover that extends upward from five thousand feet, so the big melt has not gotten underway yet. Some strangers have come to sail down the Colvos Passage by Vashon Island, although they don't call it that. In fact, this day they do not recognize it as an island at all. They are making a map, and place names have not yet been assigned. Vashon has still not been charted.

The year is 1792, three centuries after Columbus found the ocean route to Cathay. George III, who has failed in his recent bid to hold on to the American colonies is still on the throne of England, as he will be for another 38 years. The Terror rages in France, murdering ten thousand innocent Frenchmen every year, foretelling the bloody Holocaust of every leftist movement that will follow. Catherine the Great rules in Russia where she hired the American naval genius, John Paul Jones, a few years ago to help her fight the Sultan's Navy in the Black Sea. She fired Jones in 1788, for irritating one of her lovers, the great Potemkin, and now he has died in Paris, just the month before. It is three years since the shock of the mutiny on the H.M.S. Bounty, and new regulations require at least two ships for long voyages such as this one. The Admiralty will not take chances like that again.

George Washington is in his first term as President of the young nation of the United States. He knows that the victory over Britain, like the new country it created, might be just a footnote in history. It is a truce, and an uneasy one at that. The military power of America's ally, France, is weakened, her finances have collapsed and her intentions are uncertain. The alliance is defunct, so now the United States is alone, as she will so often be in the future.

The visitors, sailing in a small launch and a cutter have entered the Colvos Passage from the north end. It seems a likely place to investigate. They do not know what is ahead, but they know exactly what they are looking for: the water route to the St. Lawrence. The Northwest

Passage.

Captain George Vancouver is not yet 35 years old, but he will die in only five years. He is a trusted officer and a seasoned explorer, a veteran of two voyages with the famous Captain James Cook, who taught him cartography. As the most capable disciple of England's most famous navigator, Vancouver is a natural to handle this critical mission. His country's future is at stake.

When Britain is able to move goods and armies across the American continent by water she will be able to stymie and encircle the United States. With her expected Indian allies, who Captain Vancouver now courts with good will and trinkets here in the Northwest, Britain will easily achieve her strategic objective. The little experiment of the Americans will soon be at an end.

Mr. Puget and Mr. Whidbey, in launch and cutter, have three days to find the end of this little passage or return with the news that it is more extensive than thought. The boats are well armed: the launch, a large open rowboat, has two swivel cannon as well as muskets and some short-barreled musketoons. The little armada has provisions for seven days – just enough to sail away for three days and then return, with one day's spare provisions to meet unexpected delays.

As they proceed down the Colvos they see Indians, but find it hard to contact them. When the visitors land at Olalla Bay they frighten away two Indians who run into the forest, leaving their canoe. Mr. Puget leaves them gifts – beads, medals and other trinkets – as evidence that their intentions are friendly.

As the launch passes Point Dalco, Mr. Puget sees the full glory of Mt. Rainier for the first time, its top *"perfectly white and appeared to reach the clouds."* He has noticed it before from farther away, but this time it is much closer. It makes quite a strong impression and he notes it in his log. Continuing on past Point Defiance and entering the Narrows, the two boats are captured by the tidal flood which *"came so strong that all our Efforts could not make way against it."*

The maps that Captain Vancouver is creating on this expedition

PROLOG

will became the mainstay of northwest coastal navigation for the next century. Unfortunately for King and Country, he finds, to everyone's disappointment, that there really *is* no Northwest Passage south of the Bering Straight. His clear, accurate maps, which still somehow omit the Columbia and Fraser Rivers, leave no doubt that the Northwest Passage was just wishful thinking.

Eleven years on, in 1803, another President, Thomas Jefferson, will make a deal with cash-strapped Napoleon Bonaparte for Louisiana, doubling the size of the United States at a single stroke. Only two years after that, Lewis and Clark will stumble, hungry and tired, out into the mouth of the Columbia River and recognize the Pacific Ocean, starting the American westward expansion that continues today.

But on *this* day, a warm day in May, in the year 1792, the glory of discovery is to Britain and the Northwest passage is just around the bend. Two young officers in His Majesty's Navy sail by Vashon Island and ride the Narrows flood.

Later, you and I will kayak there. It will be fun.

The faultfinder will find faults even in Paradise

Thoreau

Beginning

I will be dead in under three minutes, and it's really annoying. My eyes feel the cold salty water and want to close – possibly for good. Confused, disoriented and feeling miffed at my sudden clumsiness, I hang upside down from the spray skirt. My instruction manual, "How to Kayak," tells me that I have to avoid panic to save my life. The best way to do that is to slowly, deliberately count to three while at the same time thinking of something useful to do.

"One."

No, no, no, no, no!!! I'm not ready to die!!! Help me!!!

Trapped upside down, I have to release the spray skirt to exit the boat. I expect to gulp the most delicious lung full of moist air I've tasted since the time I was sucked to the bottom of the Rio Grande after my brother talked me into jumping into deep rapids for a swim.

"Pull forward on the tab, then up," say the clear instructions in "How to Kayak."

"Two."

Though the green murk I can make out the bright yellow loop at the front of the spray skirt. I reach forward and with all my panic-induced hyper strength I pull up. That's an ineffective strategy though, since I forget to pull *out* first. Yanking again even harder I somehow manage to force the bungee off the coaming and I am free.

I taste the delicious air. Then I taste defeat.

I am out of the upside-down kayak but I am floating in the frigid water. Now I will be dead in *thirty* minutes. This time from hypothermia. My former ride is now my burden. I have to rescue not only myself, but the boat, too. Full of water and very heavy, she floats low and muddles about in the choppy wake surf.

This is my first day – actually my first five minutes – with my brand new kayak, so I have not anticipated having to rescue myself this soon. I still have not received my paddle float and bilge pump, or even ordered them yet. I am more or less M.I.A. in the self-rescue department.

Looking at the distance to shore, I figure I can swim for it. With luck I will make it before mortality sets in. But as I assume the position in preparation for my exhausting dog paddle and boat tow I notice that my neoprene-covered feet strike a hard object. It is, as turns out, the sea floor. At low tide, we refer to it as the "beach."

Soggy, shivering, and unheroically covered with an unknown greenish slime I wade back to dry land, towing my low-riding, upside-down kayak, as nonchalantly as possible. Standing on the rocky shore, I lift the bow and dump her sad, guilty contents into the Sound.

With the sudden clarity of a cherry bomb in church, I understand at this moment that I am not now nor ever have been a kayaker. I am just a book reader with unrealistic expectations. To kayak is to drown. I am going to get a book on something else.

$$\Omega$$

It is a year and more later. The October morning is gray and cool. Drizzle is expected but just at the moment the air is clean and calm. The water is as flat and perfect as a skating rink right after the Zamboni. I finish my hasty breakfast, planning my morning as I would plan to photograph a moonrise. Timing is everything.

My tide window is very short this day. The beach appears and disappears in only about three hours. I can't get into the boat with no beach, and with no beach I can't get out of it. I can't leave early, and if I come back late...

On my deck, feeling a rising energy of anticipation, I quickly do the familiar preflight. Paddles, paddle float, bilge pump, sponge, water bottle in the boat. Spray skirt, PFD, hat and wrist GPS on me. I schlep my forty-two pound kayak down the steep stairs and set it on the narrow shelf of wet gravel. I stand on the beach and smile as I ready my gear.

Barnacles cover the small stones of our beach. The stones are remnants of the glacier's passage not so long ago. Where I stand the ice was more than a kilometer thick. It flowed inexorably for a hundred centuries and ground all the rocks underneath into smooth red-potato shapes. Nearly round, but not quite. Global warming melted the ice. People came. They invented fiberglass. They made kayaks.

Our ferry, the Rhododendron, moves out of the slip with a stately stride. Fast, without the appearance of speed, it has nearly sent more than one intoxicated fisherman or brazen teen boater to the bottom. It is green and white. It holds forty-eight cars, but has only a few this Sunday morning. Most people are still at home, so I have the world to myself.

I take care to snap the paddles together properly. I am a no-feather guy, so I use the middle button hole. I lift the boat by both ends of the coaming and gently place it in the shallow water, away from the larger rocks. I tuck the back of my spray skirt up into my PFD so I won't sit on it when I get in the boat. I stand in the water and using the paddle as an outrigger I squat down to sit on the coaming. I lift my right leg and let the water run off the sole of my bootie, then put my leg into the boat. Left foot hung to dry and leg in, I put feet to pegs and push off with the paddle.

Just a short trip down to Quartermaster harbor and back. That's all I have time for today.

Paddling is a chore at first as I warm up my muscles. My left shoulder always takes a while to come on line. I tell myself that I am doing fine for a 59-year-old man. Nearer the end than the beginning, but it still feels like the beginning of something every day. This day, the day of the story, has an ineffable magic to it. Something is very right.

There are terrible rocks at Neil Point and I must pass them. The bigger ones are the size of a Yugo. I have named one of them the "Point Rock." When I can see it I know where safety is and where danger is. This day, the water is still too high to see the Point Rock. Occasionally before I have been surprised, paddling at full speed, to look down and see a massive boulder, thickly matted with razor-sharp barnacles, pass inches below my hull. A kayak needs space to stop. Rocks ahead can't be seen, they must be avoided. I aim more to the south, giving the Point Rock plenty of room to hide under the water.

The clouds are low this day, but on other days, when the air is clear, I can see the full face of Rainier from here. It is almost exactly fifty miles to the summit, but three miles high, so big that it looks much closer.

As I paddle around the point and into the shelter of Quartermaster, I see no other boats and no people on the narrow beach. A deer grazes, ignoring my visit. Gulls scream, chase and threaten each other. There are no friends among them. One of them has a clam. He flies fifty feet into the air and drops it on the rocks. It breaks open. He dives behind it to protect it from his greedy fellows. Pulling out the living meat, he shakes it to show who's boss.

Gray skies are reflected in the still water. The brilliant greens of the bluffs are muted in the filtered light. There are only a few houses here. One has lights on, but the others are dark. Maybe the owners live in the city and haven't come on this gray day.

When the water is flat and there is no wind, a kayaker seems to float on nothing. Paddling is flying. If I stop working, the bow wake shows my glide progress for a long time like the trail of a waterbug in a horse trough. Each new stroke of the paddle brings a joy that the runner can not know. It is gentle, like the beat of an eagle's wing. It is powerful. It is easy. My lungs, my back, my legs, my arms, my joyful mind all fly together. We are of the boat. We are the boat.

The sun is still low and the water clear. I see black sand dollars on the sandy bottom just a couple of feet below me, stacked like chips at Vegas. A flounder kicks up a siltstorm escaping my shadow. Eelgrass waves as he passes. Later I float over a small shark, a dogfish, wagging its tail.

Imperceptibly, the flat water changes as long rollers overtake me, the decrepit wake of a distant container ship that entered the Port of Tacoma an hour ago. A light drizzle falls on the windless water and the low rollers are instantly textured with tiny craters. The boat rises, falls and flies. Electric pleasure pounds my heart. It sings like the stays on a schooner in a gale.

Becoming

I learned to kayak on Vashon at Jensen Point in 1996, before the Burton Acres Boathouse was built. Doug Baum used to trailer his rental boats to the Point and meet customers there on Saturday and Sunday. Vashon Island Kayaks was a no-frills operation, but a good one. Customers had fun then, and they still do today.

My wife, my brother and I all wanted to paddle, and what Doug suggested was a single and a double. My wife and I took the double and my brother grabbed the single. None of us had a clue what to do other than what Doug had showed us in his orientation.

A double kayak takes teamwork. The person in the rear seat handles the rudder. A rudder in a kayak is usually not needed, but that is probably the only way you can control a double. Two experienced kayakers could get by without it, I suppose, but two novices would definitely flounder. We were not to the novice point yet.

Doug's white fiberglass double was heavy and hard to carry from the trailer to the beach. Fortunately, at Jensen Point, the trip is short. Doug showed us the 90° method which is where the boat is pointed perpendicular to the beach. That makes launch a bit more strenuous but more likely to succeed. Beginners can easily roll the kayak trying to get it into the water. Rolling onto rocks is painful, and the 90o method makes that less likely, since you are already pointed in the direction you want to go.

We faced down the gentle dangers of Quartermaster Harbor and began paddling around in a haphazard fashion. We tried racing, but that took more coordination than my wife and I could muster. Alone in his NC-17, my brother had no problem crushing us in every contest.

Coordinating a double kayak is easier if the two team members paddle in unison. Left, right, left, etc. If they do not get the rhythm, then they constantly drip on each other. We were getting wet. My brother was clearly having a better time of it.

The rental was paid for four hours, but we were ready for lunch, cold and wet. Our arms were killing us. Not understanding how to paddle a kayak, all three of us just used our arm muscles until they were finished. A trained paddler uses his whole body – back, legs, chest and shoulders, but that takes a little practice and training. Beginners never think about how to paddle. It seems so obvious.

We quit after only two hours that day, feeling that we had seen what there was to see and done what there was to do. "I thought there would be more," I remember thinking. "It's nice, but what's so special about it?"

Now I go every day, but after my first day in the double I waited a year before I tried again. I did not see the thrill. My wife never got back in a kayak. There was nothing there for her. In fact, for her, like for many people who really don't enjoy being on the water, there is nothing for her in any boat. She rides the ferry every day and that is enough.

After a year of festering, I decided to try the kayak again. This time in a single, and by myself. The Mrs. had other plans. I made the appointment with Doug, got the orientation, signed the release and was ready to go.

Doug wanted me to try a maneuverable boat with no rudder. I couldn't imagine how it would be possible to control a rudderless kayak, so I insisted on renting one with rudder. Doug sighed in resignation and brought out an old clunker instead of the prize boat he had tried to put me in. Pearls before swine.

At the time I did not understand why some people don't think kayaks need rudders. Instead of adjustable fixed pegs that allow your knees to securely engage the inside of the hull, your feet are necessarily free to move. That means they can't be in the same place all the time, and that means that your knees can't control the roll. Not being able to properly control the roll means that the boat is sloppy. A sloppy boat is not under control, rudder or no rudder.

As a pilot I was comfortable with moving rudder pedals as a means of controlling the boat. To my unsophisticated mind, it just seemed natural. Now, after years of kayaking, I don't see it that way anymore.

Doug helped me carry the boat to the water, reminded me again how to enter and exit, then quickly lost interest in me as I struggled away across the stony beach. Other customers were arriving, and he had held my hand long enough.

I was on my own. My first solo.

Now, whenever I paddle around Jensen Point, the area seems quite benign, but those days everything was new and unfamiliar. I stayed pretty close to shore not knowing if I would really be able to rescue myself should the need arise. There was some chop that July day, from wakes and wind. When a person first starts to paddle, or when he gets into a new boat for the first time, he really doesn't know what the parameters are.

A good kayaker can keep his upper torso vertical while rolling the boat with his knees. You can roll the boat as far as you can bend at the waist with no danger of rolling over, as long as your weight is still centered. If your head is not above the boat's center of mass you enter the danger zone. Leaning your upper body past the tipping point results in an immediate roll. So it's like skiing. You need to let your lower body move around for control, but your upper body remains calm and erect for balance.

These are things I did not know at the time.

I knew that if I "screwed up" I would go into the cold water and have a choice between swimming for shore and trying to re-enter the boat using the paddle float – something I had neither attempted nor witnessed. I really doubted I could do it. Later, after Doug gave me the rescue class, I realized that I probably could *not* have done it, and my only option would have been to swim for shore or holler for help.

I decided to brave the choppy waters and make for Dockton. It's about a mile from Jensen Point to Dockton Park, a fifteen minute paddle at cruising speed in a decent boat. At the time the distance seemed impossible, even though it's all sheltered and the actual area of open water is quite short. But as a beginner, I had no feel for the scale and no way to know how long it would take. You are never very far from shore except when out in the middle, but I could not really tell how far out the middle was. It was my first open water crossing and in the chop and wind it seemed a brazen thing to do.

Twenty minutes of sweaty work got me to Dockton. I could have landed there, but there didn't seem to be any reason, since the facilities are certainly no improvement over Jensen Point. No cup of tea, cappuccino or fresh pastry is on offer at either place. The beach at Dockton is mud instead of rocks and while the park there is quite nice, I was not there to visit the park. I was out for a paddle, and paddle I would.

The water was gray and brown that day, since it was cloudy and the surf stirred up the bottom. Things were moving faster than I expected. I had to paddle hard to get to Dockton. I had to paddle hard to get back. The waves were frightening, but the harbor was full of power boats, sailboats and other kayaks. People were enjoying themselves everywhere. It did not seem like a survival situation.

I had taken it to the edge – my edge, that is, and it was Fun. It was really Fun. Why had I never tried this before? Man gets in a boat, goes out in the water and comes back alive. Yee Ha!!! Now that's Fun.

So that's how it all got started. Not the day with the wife and the brother, but the day when it was just me, paddling a sloppy kayak with no clue how to do it, in choppy gray water. I made it there, and I made it back. I was hooked.

Those days, Monday mornings were killer. 3 a.m. wake up call, Vashon Shuttle pickup at 3:30, the 4:05 boat, then a 6 a.m. flight to the east coast. Back home on the last boat Friday night. Make that Saturday morning. There was no time to think about kayaks or anything but work.

Now it's a year later and I have not been in a kayak again since the Amazing Crossing of Quartermaster Harbor the previous summer. I can feel the kayak thing festering again and I say to the wife "I think I'll buy a kayak."

So I started asking around, looking at kayaks in the neighborhood and trying to figure out how to buy one. At first it was overwhelming. There were so many choices and so many options. Plastic, fiberglass, rudder, two place, sit-on-top...

At the time I did not understand any of that. I didn't know the important from the fluff, the necessary from the burdensome. I just knew a few people who had their own boats, and, one I kept seeing looked like it might work for me. It was built locally, in Tacoma.

If you can find a local manufacturer, your life is easier. You can go there in person, see their setup, see their inventory, talk calmly about options and just get a feel for the outfit. You can even decide if you like them personally, which may be important.

When dealing with a local manufacturer there are three ways you might be able so save a considerable amount of money. First, you can pick the boat up yourself at their factory which means your shipping costs go to zero. Second, you may be able to purchase a blemished, or factory-second boat which will be discounted from list price. Third, you may be able to buy at wholesale, which is a real markdown.

I found NC Kayaks in Tacoma. Doug and Greg were great to talk to and I think their boats are excellent. I was worried about weight, since I have to climb about sixty feet down to the beach. I wanted a 17-foot boat, since that is a good size compromise, and I wanted to be able to carry it up and down steep, tricky steps by myself.

Their NC-17 Daytripper comes in a low-weight version that weighs only 42 pounds. Compare that with an 80-pound plastic boat of the same size, and it seems extremely light. I have since met someone who told me she has a Kevlar boat, a 28-pound sixteen-footer. I've never seen a boat that light, though, and I don't know who makes them.

The NC Kayaks factory is located on Chandler Street in Tacoma. My wife and I had a hard time finding Chandler Street, which is off Center Street, in an industrial neighborhood. Greg showed me around the shop which was full of kayaks in various stages of completion. We had chatted on the phone before I came. He had a blemished boat that he wanted to show me.

It was a lime green NC-17 Daytripper that was almost complete. It had a paint blemish, so he was offering it at a reduced price. We made the deal, contingent on Greg delivering the boat to me on Vashon – I still had no way to carry it. He wanted gas money and a ferry ticket.

"Done."

"I'll call you when it's ready."

Back in the truck, we headed for home. I had a kayak.

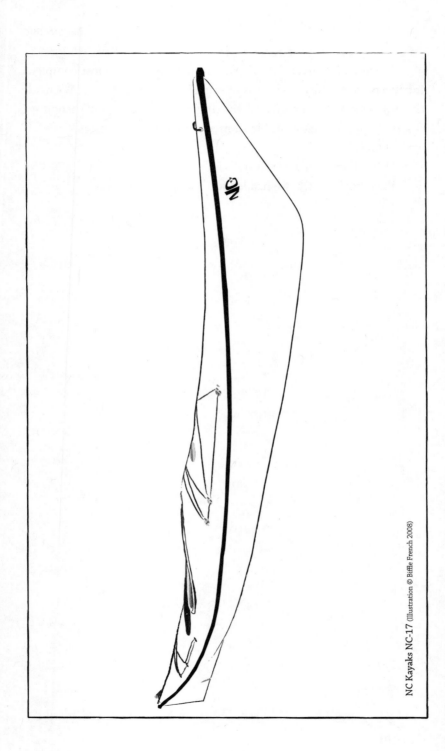

NC Kayaks NC-17 (Illustration © Biffle French 2008)

The Boat

It is a few days after my visit to NC Kayaks. The deal is done, Visa has said "Yes" to what everyone clearly knows is a completely frivolous charge and I wait for the call.

"It's ready," says Greg's voice on the phone. "I'll be over on the Rhody sometime this afternoon. You gonna be there?"

I have told fifty lies to spend this week on Vashon instead of New York City. "Oh yeah, I'll be here."

I watch the boat leave Point Defiance and scoot across to the Tahlequah dock. I stare at the driveway like a snake stares at a mouse. His little car manages the steep hill OK, but looks like it is barely big enough to carry the seventeen-foot boat. He seems unconcerned as we slide it off his roof rack. I can see that I'll need something like that myself pretty soon. In the event, however, I will discover plenty of kayaking on south Vashon and just paddle around Tahlequah for over a year.

We each grab a carry handle and carefully haul my new prize down twenty steps to the cedar deck. I look at the lime green boat and experience that mushy feeling of a high school boy gazing on his brand-new steady girl friend. I feel that same unabashed sexual infatuation and proprietary pride that I used to get from knowing those big boobies were for me. Now, as then, I'm thinking "Let's go for a *ride!!!*"

I have been reading "How to Kayak" every day now since my trip to NC Kayaks. I'm pretty sure I have the whole thing figured out. I know which accessories I still need to buy, but Greg brings me the basic starter kit: boat, paddle, spray skirt. The skirt is already fitted to the coaming and paddles are pretty generic. Except for a rescue kit, I am ready to rock and roll.

It's late in the afternoon this March day and I have to join a conference call. Greg and I chat a bit. "Watch out for the tides." he tells me. "Make sure you can get back. Sometimes people get stuck out at high tide and get in trouble."

"Oh yeah. I got all that figured out. I'll be fine."

I go inside, sit at my desk, dial the access number and try to pay attention. I am supposed to be the expert, but I keep fading out and everybody knows I am somewhere else. I resolve to do better next time.

The tide is high the next morning, a day full of expectation and cool breezes. My next good tide window is in the afternoon. I struggle all day at the computer and phone, planning my getaway. About 2 p.m. I make the first of hundreds of trips down my steep steps, carrying the new boat on my shoulder. Picking a sandy spot in the scupper delta, I practice getting in and out of the boat.

There is a creek gurgling from deep inside the Vashon aquifer that used to discharge directly onto the beach before our road was constructed. When the road was put in, sometime in the 1940s, a drainage ditch was dug to collect the stream water. A drain pipe, or scupper, was installed to empty the drainage ditch and keep the stream flowing to the beach. These are everywhere on Vashon, and everywhere else for that matter. Without them, no roads could ever be built on any hilly spot.

The stream cascading down the steep hill is full of silt which also fills the ditch and runs into the scupper with the water. At the mouth of the scupper there is a sandy delta where the stream used to empty, and where the scupper now empties its silty brew. That is the scupper delta. The rest of the beach is covered with pebbles or boulders. But here, in the scupper delta, it is sandy. A good place to start kayaking. The sun has come out. I feel like I'm in Heaven.

I wish I had ordered my rescue kit, but there are so many things to learn right now and rescue is way down the list. I have to practice getting in and out, paddling, turning – my first time to try paddling a boat without a rudder. Correspondence school kayak instruction.

I put the boat parallel to the beach in six inches of water, steady it with the paddle held firmly perpendicular to the coaming and resting on the beach. I sit down on the side. There is a wake hitting the beach as I start this maneuver, and that makes it a little more difficult. The boat rises, climbs the beach, falls, leaves the beach. I am chasing it. I decide to wait until the wake passes. Calm seas again, right foot in, left foot in, both feet on the pegs, I push off and I am free.

The boat moves easily, but I am still learning to control it. I paddle straight with no trouble, but turning is harder. Let's see, do I roll right to turn left or is it the other way?

The correct way is to roll away from the turn, just the opposite of an airplane. You take the bow and stern, which are shaped for straight tracking, out of the water and put the boat onto the rounded surface of the hull side. It's kind of like skiing a mogul. Centers of the skis at the top of the mogul, turning is easy. Tips of the skis in the trough, it's harder.

So for a right turn, you roll the deck of the boat to the left, paddle on the left side and you will turn right. The farther you roll the boat, the easier it is to turn, and the faster as well. I start to practice this. It feels a bit clumsy and sloppy, since I really don't have my knees locked into the top of the hull very well, but at least I think I understand the theory. I turn right. I turn left. *Yes!!!* I am doing it.

Now, maybe if I could roll just a little bit farther, I could turn a little faster. Let's see, just lean over here a bit and...Hey!!! Whoa!!! Help!!!

Rolling the kayak into a turn is done with the knees and hips, but I have done it with head and shoulders, which is fatally bad form. I reach and pass the tipping point without a care, completely oblivious to what is happening to me. It is like doing a gentle aileron roll, except for the part where it suddenly stops half way around. Now I am upside down. This is no good. I have really done it this time.

I will be dead in three minutes or so. "A kayak," she will say, "yes, that's right. Now about that insurance..."

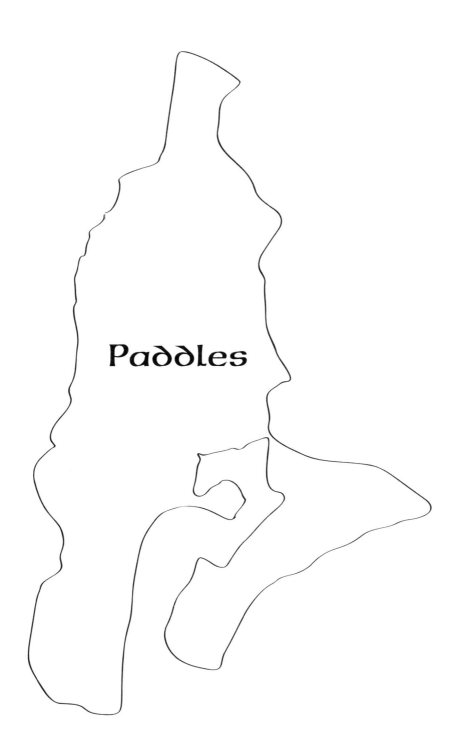

Those who control their passions do so because their passions are weak enough to be controlled.

William Blake

Paddles

Any paddle may turn out an adventure. When you and I put our kayaks into the water, we never know what is going to happen. We are like the weatherman: the only thing we can say for sure is that we really don't know for sure. Sometimes a paddle is a workout—sometimes it is a religious experience, but when you slide into the cockpit of a wet kayak and strike out into cold blue or gray salt water you have no idea which it will be.

I tried to break some ground for you by paddling every bit of coastline on Vashon. For the intrepid, this might be the work of a day. For me it took the whole summer. I had to revisit old paddles to refresh my memory, and explore new ones for the first time. They are all here, though, and I hope you like them.

These paddles are my offering to you. I held them for a while, now I am passing them on. Maybe you were there many times already, or maybe you are still waiting to go, no matter—now you will know the way.

There are cautionary tales here, too. I try not to put myself into danger knowingly, but sometimes it has happened through my own ignorance or sloppiness. I hope you can learn something from my failures and tough lessons, and that these tales will guard you from the stupid mistakes I made. For a lot of people I can't expect it, of course – many of us only learn the hard way.

Except for you, that is. I know you are smarter than that.

Rounding Point Dalco on the Flood

I learned to paddle in Maine. Out there the fishermen call kayakers "speed bumps." David Shull

One of my favorite paddles is just around Point Dalco from Tahlequah. Don't try to paddle here on the ebb tide because the current is too strong against you and you will have a hard time getting past the rips. But on the flood it is like paddling a lake, the water clear and calm, the boat easy to manage. Today is like that, tame as a lamb. It is a neap flood tide, the easy time to round Dalco.

Today is August 21st. Summer is still here, but today is cloudy and cool. It is drizzling, and a cool mist coats me as I walk outside. I make the mistake of putting on my Polartec shorty, figuring that I will be cold in just a T-shirt.

A blue heron stands sentinel on my beach, as she does every morning. The big birds respect each other's territory and even mates do not fish together. Her long legs and neck remain still until a meal approaches, then she strikes like a snake. She seems never to miss.

Fog rises from the water in little fog mountains and curls in wisps across the far shore. The green and white Rhododendron, our little ferry, appears silently out of it like a levitating wraith, heading for Tahlequah. She docks and begins to offload with two large clanks for every vehicle. I carefully paddle by, well out to sea, giving the Rhody a wide berth and making sure the crew sees me. One of them waves.

I used to wait for the ferry to leave, trying to be as safe as possible. A good friend is a deck hand on the Rhody, and I mentioned it to him one day in conversation.

"Just go under the bridge. I do it all the time. It's legal. They don't care," he said.

The ferry slip is a big, complex machine with large moving parts and a massive structure that holds it all together. There is a long stationary bridge linking Vashon Highway to the slip itself. The slip consists of several elements.

There is a movable drawbridge that allows the crew to adjust for the tide swing, which may be as much as 17 feet during the year, high high water to low low water. The drawbridge is supported by big steel cables that drop down from a large frame called a "transfer span." A powerful electric motor turns a capstan that takes up the cables through pulleys on the transfer span and lifts the drawbridge. During loading and unloading operations, the drawbridge rests on the boat deck, which takes up most of the load.

When the ferry docks, the deckhands grab two-inch diameter, woven polyester lines that are tied to the slip and they casually wind them around the big cleats on the boat deck. That's supposed to keep the boat from drifting away from the slip, but what really holds it in position is the propulsion from the screws.

The ferry does not really have a reverse. Instead, it goes forward in both directions. There is no bow and no stern, just "End No. 1" and "End No. 2."

We refer to the Rhody as our "little" ferry, and, compared to the behemoths of the fleet, it is rather small. But compared to my kayak it is a mountain. The little ferry is 237 feet long, 62 feet wide and has a car deck clearance of nearly 14 feet. It draws 10 feet of water. The Rhody's two 2,172 horsepower diesel engines propel it at 11 knots fully loaded—double my sprint speed. It grosses 937 tons, just under 10,000 times the combined weight of my kayak and me. I am no match for it.

If the Rhody faces "forward" into the slip, then I am passing "behind" it. The thrust from the idling diesels that holds it in place creates a powerful current behind it, enough to spin a kayak, regardless of what the paddler does. That is why I pass well seaward of it. It is the prudent thing to do, and I always *try* to be prudent even if sometimes I just don't think it completely through.

I pass behind the Rhody today because I have a burning mem-

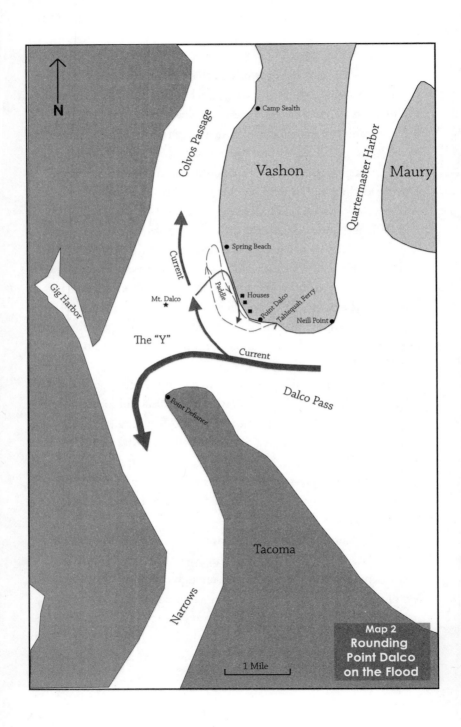

ory of the time I took the other course. After talking with my friend, I had an easy route past the slip. I could always go underneath, and what a cool place to be. Looking up at the bottom of the green steel drawbridge with the reflections of the choppy water playing on it, I was reminded of how my brothers and I used to play in a big culvert pipe near the ranch as kids. Only here there are no crawdads, no water moccasins, just the odd pigeon guillemot.

Coming home from rounding Point Dalco a year or so ago, I found my path blocked by the Rhody. "It's legal. They don't care," rang in my ears. They were still loading, so I thought I had plenty of time. I glanced up just in time to see the last car roll on. Suddenly the deckhand buttoned up the rear stanchions, fastened the chains and the boat began to move.

With no more warning than that, a frightening maelstrom formed directly in front of my kayak as the Rhody reversed her screws and began to power out of the slip at full throttle. Gently, she moved away, behind her a deadly, swirling rapid.

I saw myself being forced sideways into the bridge pilings at high speed. I back paddled furiously, screaming words people couldn't say on TV until I was already grown up. Somehow, using all my power and skill, I rescued myself from being plastered like a discarded piece of pink bubblegum on barnacle-covered, creosote-impregnated tree trunks sticking out of 20 foot deep water. It would not have been pretty.

"A kayak. Yes, that's right. Oh yes, very sad. Now about the insurance..."

So now I never pass under the drawbridge. I may scoot by near the landward end of the car bridge, in two feet of water, or pass by well to seaward if I think I have time. Sometimes I just wait.

Today is a salmon fishing day for many people, mostly middle-aged men in specially-equipped boats. They cluster around Point Dalco and I scoot through them carefully. It is pretty safe when there are so many boats, since everybody knows it is a crowded area and while trying to avoid each other they usually can't fail to spot a nearby lime-green kayak.

In this gentle flood tide there are no rips. In general, when there is fog, as there is today, there is no wind. Fog can't form well in wind. I love to kayak on days when there is a little fog, because I know the weather will be easy. With no current and no waves except for a few rollers left by the wakes of the fishing boats, I have that flying feeling again today.

I'm getting sweaty in my Polartec, since it is now about 60° and the misty rain has stopped – it was a poor fashion choice. I unzip both my PFD and Polartec down to my navel, which gives some relief.

I'm through the cluster of boats now, around the point. Just around Dalco to the northwest there are some houses. Two of them are starting to go to ruin, but one is a well-used place that is beautifully kept. It is still alive. None of the three has access from the road which is far above, behind a tall, sheer bluff.

The living house is painted a bright yellow. It has a couple of outbuildings and there is a big white buoy cabled in place in front. Power lines come down the hill, over the bluff. It was here, on a boulder on the beach in front of the yellow house that I witnessed an incredible event a couple years ago.

As I paddled by, a half mile or so out to sea, in the middle of the Colvos, I could hear a dog barking loudly and insistently. There are never dogs there, so I thought I'd investigate.

As I got closer, I saw a young Husky, tail in the air, standing in the middle of a boulder barking at something else on the same little promontory. The rock was surrounded by water, and the tide was rising. Where the Husky stood was at the roundish top, and the other creature was huddled at the edge, just above the water.

Still paddling toward the confrontation I began to make out that the smaller creature was a raccoon, and he was a raccoon who was in some real pretty shit. Behind the raccoon was the frigid water. If he jumped in, the dog would never let him back on the beach. His tail was already under the surface and he could surely feel the cold. He looked defeated, the fur on his back was matted from backing too far into the water. Dog was Death, but maybe not. Maybe he still had a chance. Barking can't kill you and so far that's all Dog was doing. In a street fight, Raccoon has a few surprises.

I was close enough now, maybe ten feet away, to see the whole thing, Dog and Raccoon locked in a struggle to the death. Dog looked at me expectantly with his blue Husky eyes as I came paddling up. He wanted some encouragement, I guess, but I could not give it. He barked without letup, telling Raccoon to just go ahead and commit suicide so he could get off the shrinking rock and go home. Water had surrounded the boulder by now, and the beach was retreating.

Raccoon, however, still had some spark left and was not ready to go just yet. From time to time he would rise up, lift his neck fur, flash his sharp teeth and make a loud, growling hiss. Dog would react with a start, but just as quickly he would redouble his barking. He would not back off an inch.

I considered moving the kayak into range so Raccoon could jump on the deck, but then I started to think about what might happen after that. Raccoon and I were not friends. He didn't know me any better then he knew Dog. Once on the deck he would probably climb my face, seeking the high ground. He might want to stay there, and be willing to fight about it. *Sorry Raccoon, you will have to self rescue.*

The water was rising quite fast. I could not stay or I would miss the beach and be caught out at high tide. I could not convince Dog and I could not help Raccoon. Turning back now and then, trying to see if Raccoon had escaped or if Dog relented, I watched the standoff continue. Dog would not release his prey, nor was he brave enough for a frontal attack. Raccoon would not chance a swim. Inexorably the water rose. The rock would be underwater very soon. I rounded Point Dalco, paddling for home.

Today, as I reach Spring Beach I start to turn around, rolling the kayak as far onto its side as I can. I have seen a photo of a guy who had the boat rolled at least 45° while he sat erect, but I'm not that flexible.

45

We turn back to Tahlequah and I follow close to the shore. The water is quite clear and I can see the bottom perfectly in the five-foot-deep water. The steep underwater walls of the Colvos gorge are thick with starfish, or sea stars as they are better called. These slow-moving predators eat mussels, clams and barnacles by cracking them open very slowly, wearing out the muscle the bivalves use to hold their shells

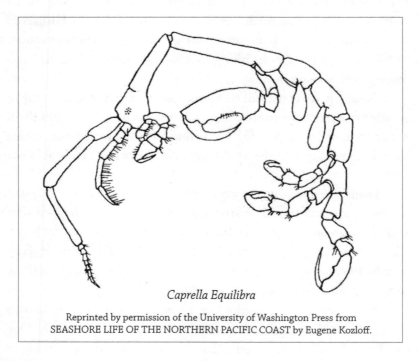

Caprella Equilibra

Reprinted by permission of the University of Washington Press from
SEASHORE LIFE OF THE NORTHERN PACIFIC COAST by Eugene Kozloff.

closed. Once inside, the sea star inserts its extendible stomach and digests the meat. Here in the clear, shallow water the army of sea stars numbers in the thousands, feeding on their helpless and countless prey. I often see them on the pilings at the ferry dock, where a few hang on during low tide, digesting a barnacle or a mussel.

Nowadays the term "sea star" is preferred to "star fish" as a way to enforce a kind of scientific political correctness—those little guys might be offended at being called "fish", as they are no such thing. I would like to point out that they are not exactly "stars", either, but then logic only carries so far.

Returning against the flood, but pulled along by a lazy favorable current in a back eddy, I float through the kelp forest just north of Dalco. The top leaves of the kelp are like flags, showing which way the current runs. The surface here is covered for a half mile or more with the plants, each lying in the same orientation, and each showing the same amount of stalk. It is a beautiful sight to see kelp laid out like this on a flat sea, somehow it's very calming.

I think there would be more kelp showing, except that the bottom falls off quite sharply here. So if there are more plants they can not reach the surface. Divers could tell me that, if I asked them, but I never have.

The kelp are in fairly deep water, but in the shallower water, near the shore, there is a forest of brown algae bushes, looking like juniper bushes under the water. My friend David, a marine biologist from the University of Washington, plucked one of the plants from the water one day. Later, on the plastic table on my deck, he showed me the plant he had picked.

"Look at this," he said, pointing to a small part of the algae bush. "Do you see that? It looks like part of the algae, but it's really a little animal. It's a Caprellid amphipod."

The creature looked like a space alien to me, but much smaller. It was maybe 1/2" in length, segmented and had a single large claw sticking out of the middle of its body that it used to grab food with. I could not see a mouth, head, stomach or any other recognizable parts. It had a special apparatus at its hindquarters for grasping the algae, its home. At first, I had trouble seeing that it was not part of the plant. Then I realized that the plant was covered with these little guys. I don't think that you could call them parasites—I think they are just free riders. The marine environment is full of fractal surprises like this. The closer you look, the more there is to see.

Nearing Point Dalco again, heading for home and work, I see the three houses. The last house, the southern one, was where I met Mike two years ago. His yellow plastic kayak was pulled up on the rotting deck, and I smelled the smoke from his hibachi. This was unusual, as I rarely see kayakers camped out like this, so I decided to pay my respects.

The old cabin once had a staircase leading to the deck, but that started to rot away years ago, and there was only a suggestion of its former presence. The tall pilings that supported the old deck beside it were still healthy, being impregnated with creosote, and the beams still looked like they might support you. The decking was mostly gone, though, and there was not much room to stand.

Under the roof of the house itself, a man in his late thirties sat on the front porch, which was still mostly intact. He was about ten feet above the beach. He was cooking something. I pulled my kayak up on the beach.

"Mornin'," I said.

"Hi there," he said. "Come on up."

The only way to do that was to climb a corroded aluminum ladder to the top of a deck beam and walk across a thin, flexing plank to the porch. I was already regretting my decision to stop by, but sometimes I just ignore that little voice that says *"Run away now, and fast!"* This was one of those times.

"Are you camping out here?," I ask.

"Well, sort of. I'm Mike. This is my dog, Sonny." He said, introducing me to a geriatric pooch of unknown breed.

Old dog eyes met mine. "I mean you no harm," said Sonny, using the time-worn doggy sign language of gently wagging his mangy tail a few times.

I once had a powerful dream that I was a world famous expert on dog body language, and ever since having that dream I have always felt like maybe I *am* a world famous expert on dog body language. Sonny and I had communicated. We were on speaking terms.

"Sonny is getting old. I found this cabin and I know a guy who is friends with the owners. We're going to turn this into, like, an old folks home for dogs and cats. I've got big ideas for this place. That way nobody ever gets put to sleep."

"Do you think King County will let you do that?," I asked, thinking that they had already decided that this one must go into the water. King County would like to demolish every waterfront structure and sue the owners for the clean up. Don't get me started on that. This one was almost gone anyway, and chances of not getting caught doing illegal repairs were zero.

"Oh sure," he said, in that dreamy way that gets my antenna up. You know, that way some people have of talking that lets you know they are from the Other Side. *King County is no problem at all for a guy who has discussions with space aliens every day, is it Sonny?*

Mike was cooking his breakfast over a fire that was really not burning all that well. He had selected green wood, which is a plentiful, but poor, fuel, owing to it being over 50% water. Green wood goes out right away unless you cook the water out first, like by pouring burning gasoline on it. Thankfully, Mike did not have any gasoline. So he had a smoking fire, and on that smoking fire he was trying to cook up some soggy frozen fried potatoes for himself and Sonny.

Now that I was fully apprised of the situation and had paid my respects, I looked at the worn out, dented aluminum ladder and flexing bridge with new eyes. Nervous eyes. I was ten feet in the air on a failing structure, and I was starting to want down.

"That's great!," I said. "I know it's going to work out for you. Gee, look at the time. I'd really like to stay and chat, but I've absolutely got to be going."

"You want some breakfast? I've got plenty."

"Uh... no thanks. I already ate. Can't paddle on an empty stomach, you know. Nice meeting you, though. I know this is going to be great here. Can't wait to see you in full swing."

I gingerly crossed the plank and carefully started down the shaky ladder. At this point I had no confidence in Mike's engineering. People from the Other Side are not always good engineers.

"That's a real nice kayak." Mike said.

"Yeah, thanks. I love it myself. It's a great boat."

Mike's yellow kayak was there on and off for a few more days, although I never saw him or Sonny again. That's been a couple of years ago already, but today, as I pass the shack, I imagine seeing the two of them up there like they were on that day, perched on that disintegrating old deck, cooking soggy frozen fries over a cold fire.

Sonny's words come back to me. "I mean you no harm."

QUARTERMASTER HARBOR

From Tahlequah a right turn takes you west, around Point Dalco. A left turn takes you east, into Quartermaster Harbor. The two paddles, so close to each other, could not be more different.

Dalco Pass is deep, open, and often violent with whirlpools, waves and wakes. It is full of fishing boats, sailboats, cruisers and sometimes tugs and barges. Quartermaster is shallow, closed, usually quiet. Boats in the harbor are smaller, fewer and slower. Often I am the only craft of any description floating in outer Quartermaster Harbor. I always share Dalco Pass and sometimes it is downright crowded.

Quartermaster is a wonderful place to see birds. In the fall and winter there are ducks of every description, cormorants, grebes, loons and many others. Spring through fall, and sometimes through the winter there are eagles there.

I have seen an eagle resting in a tree above the beach who flew down and smacked the water with his talons as if he were fishing—only he wasn't. He just flew back up into the tree, sat there for a couple minutes and then did it again. He repeated this exercise maybe ten times as I watched, and it seemed to me that he was doing it for pleasure. He clearly wasn't fishing because he kept hitting the same place and never coming up with a fish. Swoop, smack, climb, land, then a brief rest. Again and again—target practice. If I were an eagle I would do that, too. What the hell.

September 1st is cloudy, cool and breezy. It is almost the end of boating season for many people, but not for me. I go anytime I can get on the beach unless the weather is iffy. I used to launch as long as the weather was not dangerous, but I had too many experiences where it got to *be* dangerous after I was already out too far, so I tightened that standard. I have more than once been in the most protected part of sweet-natured Quartermaster and seriously questioned my ability to get back home—frightening head-high waves and winds so strong I could not make forward progress tried to push me backwards to Bur-

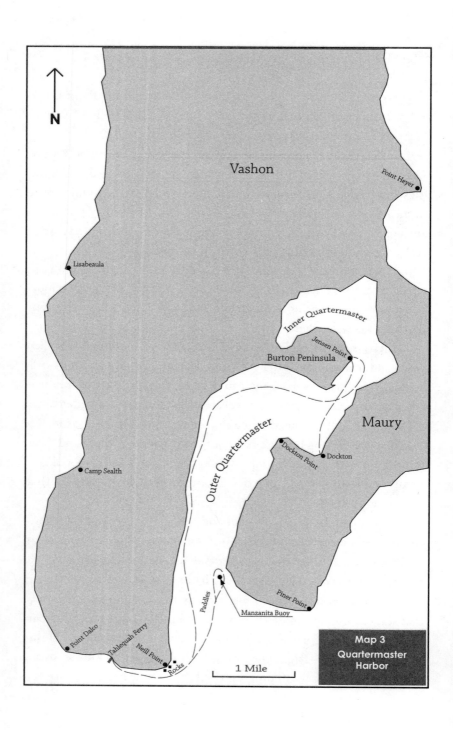

ton, where I did not want to go. Now I am more careful.

There are small waves today. That gives a ride that is not as much like flying as the calm water can be, but is still paddling and all paddling is fun. I round Neil Point, avoiding its many dangerous rocks, and head for the red Manzanita Buoy. "Manzanita" is Spanish for "little apple," probably a remnant of the orchard time, since the Spanish were never here.

The buoy is named after the little Manzanita neighborhood just nearby on Maury Island. It's one of those older beach communities with cute little houses, but no mansions yet.

I have a friend who is a tile setter. He told me that the average remodel he works on these days runs to more than $200K, almost as much as my little house cost when I bought it. Many of the little houses at Manzanita may be tiled extravaganzas on the inside. Some folks leave the outside to rot, so they can fool greedy tax assessors.

Any red marine navigation signal, like this buoy, is an indication to boaters that they should pass to the left of it when returning to a harbor. Manzanita has a dangerous shoal that extends a long way from the beach and the red buoy marks it. "Red Right Returning" is the mantra. The buoy should be on your right when you are returning to the harbor, otherwise you can end up in the shallows a long way from the beach. On a cold, windy night a boater might not make it to shore.

From my house the out-and-back to the Manzanita buoy is a four-mile round trip. It's a terrific way to get an hour's work out.

Because the harbor is such a benign environment, I do see other kayakers there sometimes. It was a breezy, sunny day in early April and I was returning from the Quartermaster when I met Chris. As I neared Neil Point I watched him paddle toward me, the wind at his back, but at my face. It was cool and gusting a bit, but there were no whitecaps and the waves were still small. It was what I guess you might call "bracing."

He was a young man, maybe thirty, paddling what looked like a brand new, bright yellow plastic kayak. He had fancy sunglasses, but no hat. His PFD was actually sort of stylish, something a grizzled old fart like me would never spend the extra money on. He had a paddle leash, which I think is unsafe, but I have to say it—he looked *flashy* in a cool sort of way.

His hair was just right, like those young guys you see on the slopes—I can't prove it, but I think some of them wear mousse. I always sport a sweat-stained old Resistol with a cork cable-tied to it. If I go in the water I want my hat back, and the cork turns it into a floater. But when I take it off, my wet hair is plastered to my scalp and I am not presentable. This fellow looked like he could pose for a TV commercial right then and there, no makeup needed.

We were two strangers on a breezy day in Quartermaster, one leaving and the other arriving. The kayak was an icebreaker, something we had in common, an excuse for a visit.

"Hidy," I said, unconsciously lapsing into Texan. I try not to do that too much around here. The locals don't reserve the same unconstrained, righteous revulsion for Texans that they hold for Californians, but they don't exactly find such a questionable origin endearing, either. When they ask me about my accent, I tell them I'm from South Vashon.

"G'day" he responded. No question about *his* accent. And no worries about taking time for a chat. Aussies are every bit as easy and outgoing as Texans. "Are there any shops up ahead?"

"There's the Burton Store up there. It's about two miles. That's the only thing around here. You could leave your kayak on the beach and walk over. It's not far to the store from the beach."

"Nice day for a paddle eh?"

"Yeah, beautiful. Kind of breezy."

"Wull, I can handle the wind, mate. It's the *current*..."

I could see the rips forming out in Dalco Pass. I figured he came from Owen Beach, so he would have to cross them to get back again.

"The tide gradient is not too steep today. I don't think the rips are going to get too bad," I offered.

"Yeah. Do you think they have tea at the Burton Store there? Two miles eh, that's the closest thing?"

"Fraid so," I said, feeling just a bit guilty for not bringing him home. It was lunchtime, but the wife is flexible where there are visitors. In Chinese a common greeting is "Did you eat yet?" and feeding a guest is the minimum standard of politeness.

It was hard maintaining position without banging into each other. We saluted and paddled on. I always wondered what stories he could have told me if I'd had him to lunch.

This day, the cloudy day in September, I am paddling for exercise. Not just for exercise but also to get my mind right. I used to treat my depression with alcohol, but that didn't work so well. I know it wasn't working because I gave it every chance for over thirty years. I mean, really, every chance. I was real good about taking my medicine. Religious, you could say.

But now I use the boat. It's a floating psychiatrist. You can not be depressed in a kayak. You can be calm, you can be angry or fearful, you can be thoughtful or you can be ecstatic, but you can *not* be depressed.

The Manzanita buoy is about 4 or 5 feet tall, as measured above the water. It is covered with guano and often there are gulls or cormorants sitting there when I arrive to make my loop around it. They always fly away when I approach, nervous about any critter bigger than they are. Cormorants still do not know that kayakers do not eat them, and they are not taking any chances.

As I approach the marker from the south, I see a racing scull approaching from the north. My position in the boat is facing forward, but the scull oarsman faces backward, pulling hard.

I don't suppose he can see me, so I make a plan to handle the coming traffic congestion. My plan is to watch what the scull does and stay far enough away to let him do it – he is faster, but I am more maneuverable. If that method doesn't work, I plan to yell like the dickens when the collision looks imminent and hope he's not wearing an iPod.

As the gap closes, I see that he's not as blind as I thought, since he's wearing a mirror like those that bicyclists sometimes use. It gives him a view to the rear and keeps him from banging into the buoy or a kayaker. He passes left of the buoy and turns right, circling clockwise. I do the same from the other side. When we are about 100 feet apart, with the red marker between us and with much different speeds, we wave. He turns north and I turn south.

I imagine it must be fun to have a fast boat like that, but in really choppy water I think the slender craft would be in trouble. And then there's that looking backwards thing.

Quartermaster, like much of the Sound, and indeed most of the west coast from Baja California to the tip of the Aleutians, is populated with small, white and gray spotted Harbor Seals. These little seals are about the size of people. Mature males can get to be over 300 pounds, but many are only 150 pounds. Females are smaller still, with many mature females only reaching 110 pounds.

As you paddle about you can see their heads pop up here and there when as they surface to breathe. I always speak when I see one near me. "Hello, Mr. Seal," I say. They snort sometimes, but they really don't want to make friends.

One day, just off Neil Point, I was paddling out with the sun in my eyes and I recognized a small Harbor Seal just ahead of me, laying full afloat. She looked asleep. I stopped paddling, amazed at the situation. When a kayaker does not paddle, he makes no sound at all, and I was pointed directly at the little seal.

The gap closed, twenty feet, ten feet. I was moving maybe one mile per hour, so this happened in slow motion. Now, at five feet away the little girl's eyes opened and met mine. "I mean you no harm" I wanted to say, but I do not know the seal lingo.

Her eyes said much, though. They opened, focused then grew to double size. "What the *Hell?*" said the seal's eyes, *"Je-*sus." She dove and disappeared quickly, safe under the water. Kayakers and seals can never be friends. Kayakers *do* eat seals, and not too far from here, either.

I saw a beautiful new wooden kayak one day just by the same place where I talked briefly to the sleeping seal, outside the dreaded rocks at Neil Point. It was a handsomely-constructed stitch-and-glue boat with a perfect finish, clear varnish on the deck and green on the hull. It was quite long, a nineteen-footer I guessed, and very sleek looking. The guy paddling it had a very serious look on his face, something I don't see much on kayakers, although some of them are a bit standoffish.

As we closed I smiled and waved. "Nice boat, did you build that?"

He frowned and looked offended by the suggestion. "Of course not, I had someone build it for me. I'm going to take it on a trip. It's a touring boat."

I could *see* that it was a touring boat. I wanted to ask him more questions, but he clearly had no interest in chatting with me, and kept on paddling by, opening the gap again. I wished I could get turned around and race him, just to see if the boat was as fast as it looked, but he was too far gone, and it takes time to do a 180. Maybe he was somebody famous and figured I'd recognize him, or maybe he was somebody who really did hate Texans. Maybe he just couldn't risk a serious conversation with a paddler wearing a sweat-stained Resistol with a cork cable-tied to it – he may have thought I was from the Other Side. I'll never know. I never saw him or the beautiful green boat again.

I saw another boat later that day that was really ugly, but the ugliest thing about it was not the boat, it was the situation. It was a guy in a kayak with no seat operated by a guy with no clue.

This boat came to my neighbor from a thief. He paddled up in it to steal another neighbor's Boston Whaler, which was moored out. I don't know if the thief was a good paddler or not, since he is a night worker while I am a night sleeper. I do think it shows a lot of chutzpah for a guy to paddle out in a kayak with no seat and leave it at the scene of a boat theft.

We found the seatless kayak floated up on the beach the next morning without a paddle. We put two and two together and figured the guy probably stole the kayak as well. He was trading up.

So the blue plastic kayak with no seat sat on a bulkhead for a couple of years—no one wanted it. Then some guests came and one of the young fellows decided he'd like to try kayaking. He would try it in a boat with no seat, which means it was uncontrollable. He borrowed a paddle from a neighbor and somehow got the craft in the water.

I was horrified to see him paddle the wobbly beast far out past swimming survival distance. He looked like he would go in with every movement and he was not wearing a PFD. In fact, he was wearing blue jeans, sneakers and a T-shirt. Great attire for the beach, not so good for swimming an impossible distance in frigid water.

Somehow he managed to get back ashore. The kayak finders sold the beach house that summer and took the dangerous blue kayak with them. It is probably in their garage now, never to float again.

A thing like that, a dangerous thoughtless killer, deserves to be in a garage. It does not belong in the water.

I met one man in Quartermaster who was paddling in a dry suit, which I imagine must have been miserably uncomfortable. I asked him why, and he told me that way he didn't need to worry about self rescue—he could stay in the water a long time in the dry suit, and someone would surely pick him up. That may be so, but a kayaker is often invisible even in the boat. Out of the boat, with only a head out of water, there is no one to see and there is no one to help. Either you get back in, you swim to shore or you "move along." Every paddler should be able to get back in. Self rescue is life.

Rounding Point Dalco on the Ebb

When the tide is ebbing, it seems impossible to get around Point Dalco from Tahlequah. The powerful tidal river that flows out of the Narrows and Dalco Pass then north up the Colvos is not monotonic—it has some surprises.

A spring tide may create a high-to-low tide difference of over 14 feet, and that drop occurs in around six hours. That means there is a lot of water trying to get into or out of the Narrows. It becomes a mighty river with rogue currents that I have GPS measured at over seven miles per hour. The tide chart says five knots (5.75 mph), but I think that is an average. Try it yourself.

Mount Dalco, a rocky underwater mountain the diameter of the Burton Peninsula and several hundred feet tall, fills the Y where Dalco Pass meets the Colvos and the Narrows. The sunken sierra creates a turbulent flow at Point Dalco with currents that are faster than a kayaker can paddle. There you find violent whirlpools and standing waves that form and reform all around the point. Traveling from west to east is exciting. Traveling from east to west by the direct route is impossible —you just can't do it.

But there is a way, a fun way if you are a confident kayaker, around Point Dalco on the ebb. It is open water, not the direct route, but it will get you there. From Tahlequah you paddle southwest, directly to Point Defiance. As you reach the park, head due west and paddle directly into the center of the strong northbound current. If you stay near the middle of this flow you will easily clear Point Dalco at high speed, and can continue all the way to Point Vashon if you are of such a mind. If you pass Spring Beach you will find it hard to return to Tahlequah, but if you turn east there and follow close to the shore you will be able to ride the strong back eddy across the powerful rips most of the way back.

The days when this is the only practical route around Point Dalco are also days when it is more challenging to cover this route. When the

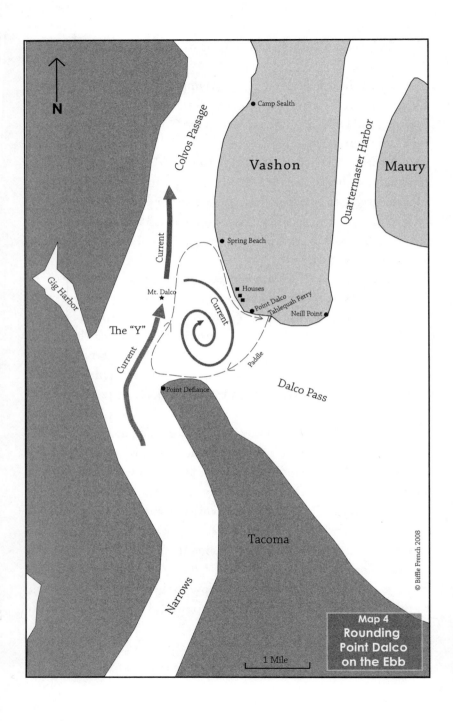

tide is high and falling, the rips are not formed. But by the time the tide gets to about seven feet the rips are powerful, and they stay that way until the flow starts to slow. You paddle across them, though, so it is not nearly as hard as pushing against the flow.

I use this route, Tahlequah to Point Defiance, around Point Dalco whenever the tide is ebbing. It is a good paddle for its own sake, and when I get into the northbound flow just west of Point Defiance I feel like I am on a rocket.

The powerful northbound flow has rips as well, of course, but there tend to be fewer back eddies in the center of The "Y" than in Dalco Pass. It is one place where the sea kayaker can just sit back and enjoy gravity drive.

When I worked in downtown Seattle for a couple of years I commuted every day on the Passenger-Only boat. We also call it the P.O. Boat, but some islanders like to contrast it with the big ferries, our car ferries. They call it the "foot ferry."

I never like to say "foot ferry" out loud around people who are not from the island, since it brings strange looks to their faces. Say it out loud: "foot ferry." See what I mean?

I commuted every day with a guy who walks with a bad limp. He almost always uses a cane and I noticed one of his legs is shorter than the other. However, he's a sturdy, athletic guy about my age, so I got to wondering what happened to his leg.

"Scuba diving," he said, "in Florida."

"How did you do that scuba diving?" Did a shark get you?"

"Nah, not a shark. A Cigarette boat.

"I was coming up from a shallow dive. My flag was out and I was right there next to it. This son of a bitch comes along, music blaring, drinking beer, joking with his buddy, ignores the flag. Never even sees me. I got chopped up by the prop. Those two assholes just kept on chugging, laughing and joking, meanwhile the water around me turned red with my blood. Just lucky there weren't any sharks that day. They'd a got me for sure."

"Man!"

Cigarette boats and their cousins, all types of "go-fast" boats are a thing to behold. Long and sleek with an enclosed bow, the pilot and a friend sit in the open cockpit on top which is maybe eight feet or so off the water and protected by a wraparound windscreen. Designed as racing boats, they have been very popular with the smuggling trade. The boat that Gong Li and Colin Farrell scooted to Havana in for the movie "Miami Vice" was a go-fast boat.

Go-fast boats run one or two unmuffled large-displacement automotive engines. They are loud enough to inhibit conversation at a distance of maybe two or three miles. Many of them can generate a thousand horsepower and make speeds of up to 80 knots (94 mph). Waterline length is around fifty feet. They are a rich man's toy and can not fail to impress.

I am on the Tahlequah to Point Defiance paddle on a warm July morning the weekend after the fourth. It is a clear blue day and the water is moving. It is ebb tide and the gradient is very steep. I am paddling to Point Defiance to meet the fast tidal current coming north out of the Narrows. I have waited until that moment when there is just enough beach to place my boat on the gravel shelf at the base of my steps. This is a trip I take whenever I can. It only happens like this in summer, and today promises to be a rocket ride.

Getting to Point Defiance from my beach takes some doing under these conditions, especially on a day like to today. First I have to cross the ferry route and stay away from the Rhody. The little ferry is fairly slow and relatively maneuverable, but he is traveling at about 12 miles an hour or so, compared with my 4, so if I get in the way it's up to him to see me, and he may not. Best to steer clear.

Once I clear the ferry route I am in the tidal currents. I get a beach when the tide hits around eight feet, and at that level the rips are not too big yet. When the tide is dropping from say plus eleven feet to minus two feet in six hours, the gradient is quite steep. Maximum flow occurs near the middle of the time between maximum high and minimum low tide. The eight foot mark, when I can launch, puts you near that time. The water is moving fast across my path.

Getting to Point Defiance can be a bit of a struggle under these conditions. The complexity of the flow causes the boat to change direction constantly during the crossing. The kayaker constantly has to adjust the track to keep a course. Eddies and whirlpools form that cause surprising momentary swings. The boat has a mind of its own.

The crossing is about two miles and I am nearly a mile from the closest land for much of it. Distances are impossible to measure when you are in the water. You really can't tell. It's "just over there," but how far is that?

This day salmon season is open. It is a Saturday, and fishing boats crowd the area of Owen beach and Point Defiance. I will have to thread the needle when I get there, but with so many boats and fishing line everywhere people are watching for each other. It's tricky, but not dangerous. Passing through a crowd like that, you can talk to people. This being Washington, though, they are surprised by it and taken aback. Texans just don't know how to act. Why *does* that boy have cork cable-tied to his cowboy hat?

But I am still in the open water a mile from the fishing area. No other boats are near me, just little dots in the distance. Like thunder in the next county, I hear a distant roar coming from the direction of Brown's Point. It grows into the unmistakable sound of a go-fast boat breaking out above the early morning din of fishing boats and the train clanking along Commencement Bay. It seems to be getting louder. I see a speck off in the distance.

As a military pilot in my twenties, I was trained to scan the horizon for dots in the distance that might suddenly grow into full-sized airplanes. When they are small, you can manage the situation. When they are full-size, you are out of options. "Keep your head on a swivel, Lieutenant. Live to be old." was my instructor's advice. Now I am old, but I want to be even older.

This distant speck has really gotten my attention. As it grows I can hear the mighty roar of twin engines putting out maximum horsepower. Soon it begins to be a defined shape, no longer just a speck. It is headed west, toward me.

I turn my boat to face him so I can see without having to turn my head around. Getting out of position like that is a good way to roll the kayak over, and I really don't want to do that in this current, especially with a go-fast bearing down on me. I want all my blood to stay in my body.

I can see that this boat is a twin hull. That is an unusual design, but it is particularly striking to me because I can now see daylight between the hulls. That can only mean he is headed straight for me. This is not a good situation and it is getting worse fast.

He does not see me. I set the boat at ninety degrees to his approach to make myself more visible. I hold my white paddle as a flag, like Custer trying to surrender to Sitting Bull and with just as much effect. I wave the paddle back and forth, but the highest point I can reach with it is still below eye level for the speeding driver's elevated perch.

I am going to get hit for sure. He is coming so fast that when he smacks me it will be all over. I am all alone out here, a mile from shore, a little spec that no one can see. I will be dead in about ten seconds.

He alters course. Not much, but maybe a degree or two. I don't see the terrifying patch of daylight between the hulls any longer. I may live.

VA-ROOOooom!!!!

Suddenly, with a roar like a top-fuel dragster passing the bleachers, he is past. The Doppler effect causes the pitch to stop increasing and begin to decrease I look up, way up, and see that the driver is not looking at me at all. His speed is at least eighty or ninety miles an hour. I have never seen a boat go that fast. He probably never saw me, and the course alteration was a maneuver he made for some other reason. Serendipity has saved me now, as so often in the past. To survive in this dangerous world takes luck more than anything else.

I am angry as hell, and I decide then and there that in future I will carry my 1911 with me when paddling. It is loaded with seven hollow points and if it doesn't jam right away I may get off a few rounds before I have to go and meet Davy Jones. I am going to have a shoulder holster fitted into my PFD. Let the water turn red with their blood, by God! No sir, I am not going down that easy!

I quickly compose a bumper sticker for the occasion: "SPEED BOATER—THIS KAYAKER IS ARMED."

Later I decide that I don't want to join the kook bumper sticker community, which thrives on Vashon as nowhere else, even with a message a timely and cogent as that one, so I drop the idea. For now, anyway.

The PFD/holster thing, now that may be something I can patent.

Tragedy

It is 6:30 p.m. on an early fall evening and I am paddling home from the Colvos when I hear a small dog barking near me on the shore. "Eek, eek, eek...."

In my mind's eye I see a Chihuahua suicidally trying to frighten a deer. I imagine this because I have just recently witnessed a terrible tragedy involving a deer and Pepi, a Shih Tzu and former neighbor.

It happened at a 12th birthday party. We adults were chatting. I was ready to scarf a big chunk of pink birthday cake with the delicious Crisco icing from Thriftway. Immediately after that I would mumble an excuse and get away from those screaming kids as soon as possible. What was I doing there, anyway?

Cautiously a doe wandered into the scene. It wasn't clear exactly what she wanted, but prize garden flowers are a deer's favorite meal, and the hostess had lovely roses planted all around the house.

"Look Mommy, a deer. Let's give him some birthday cake."

Pepi, the little Shih Tzu and a birthday present from last year found the doe's approach uncomfortably close and started warning her off with a loud bark, hoping to protect the guests.

"Eek, eek, eek..."

This very much reminded me of how my brother once taught his giant Rhodesian Ridgeback to respond aggressively to the phrase "FBI." I couldn't envision a situation where that would be helpful, but my brother is always thinking.

No one expected what happened next. The deer surged forward menopausally and grabbed the little pooch with her front legs. Scooping the frightened, squealing victim under her body, she stood full height and delivered a cruel stomp with her sharp front hooves. A shocked silence ensued. Not satisfied with a single blow, the deer stood, pointed and stomped again and again until the foul assassination was done and done well.

"Bambi killed Pepi!!! Bambi killed Pepi!!!" Shih Tzu brains and red blood stained the green grass. Three weddings and a funeral. A birthday and a murder. The doe walked away slowly, insolently. It shat a shiny black corrugated turd the size of a fat cucumber. Pepi sleeps with the fishes.

Occurrences like this one only serve to confirm the worst for those of us with a primal fear of ungulates. I have long advocated reasonable methods of deer population control based on widespread use of deer poisons, spring steel traps, bounty hunters and exploding mines placed on deer trails. However, my soft-hearted neighbors insist that "a sustainable balance is achievable that relies on natural predation by automobiles and motorcycles."

I paddle along, reliving frightful the scene, so recent and so ugly. "Stop barking, Pepi!," I think out loud. "Stop barking and run away!"

"Eek, eek, eek..."

But I suddenly realize that I have completely misunderstood. There is no Devil Bambi here to frighten little children, and no innocent Shih Tzu to sacrifice. As my airplane-deafened ears hone in on the sound, I find I am looking at a large, plastic hot tub that has been placed as close to the beach as possible. Illegal wiring powers it—quintessential Vashon engineering.

A middle aged woman and her portly companion standing in the knee-deep water are disporting themselves "doggie style," and managing it rather well. It is her soprano shrieks of pleasure I am hearing. "Eek, eek, eek...."

Pendulous breasts flop in time with the shrieks. Water sloshes over the rim. Two wine glasses, almost empty, stand at hand. Two dead soldiers and one unopened California Merlot bottle are lined up on the nearby table. Pants and T-shirts cover the chairs. A full ash tray pollutes the table-top. Steamy clouds rise from the warm water. They do not see the kayak, and there is nothing to hear. They are alone with their simple pleasures.

I look away and bend my back to the paddle. Lights come on in a house up the hill.

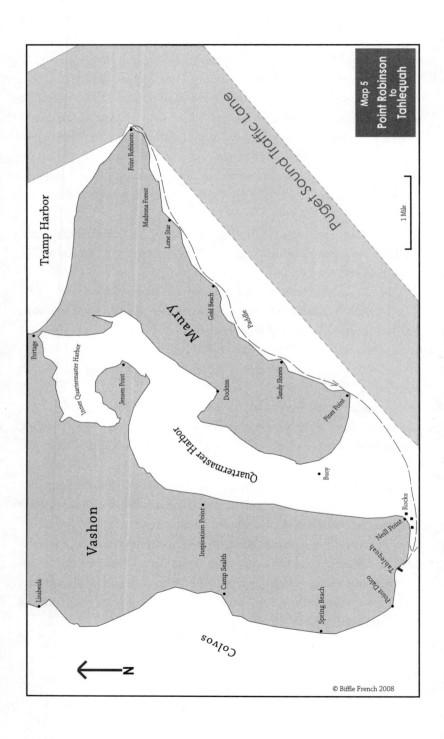

Point Robinson to Tahlequah

It's August 11th, and the weather looks perfect. Summer has been a disappointment this year, with only a few days in the 70s and lots of chilly, cloudy days. Now that it's turned out nice, everyone is outside. The salmon are running heavy and fishing boats are everywhere.

I loaded my kayak onto the roof rack on the Tacoma the night before my little trip. That way I'm ready to go early, before the parking lot gets crowded. The lighthouse and park are popular, and Point Robinson has one of the best public beaches on the island. It's a great place to launch from, or just to hang out.

I check the tide chart and see that low tide at Neil Point is 10:30 AM, but slack water is 11:30. The current only reverses at slack water, not low tide, since there is some inertia in the system. Since I will paddle off at around 8:00, I know that whatever the current is then, barring an eddy here and there, it will be that way most of the trip.

Looking at the tide schedule and the navigation chart, you'd think that the tide would be stiff against me the whole way. But because of the reduced current flow near the beach, I don't really expect it to be that bad. I'm not hoping for a tailwind, but I'm not looking for a one-knot slog either. It's eight miles from Point Robinson to Tahlequah, and if I had to fight that hard it would make more sense to spot the truck and paddle the other direction.

Breakfast done, I slip into my swim suit and a long-sleeved T-shirt. Both my brothers have had numerous skin cancers and I don't want any. I was always the one who wore the hat and used sunscreen. Now they suffer, but I am mostly whole. My rich and handsome younger brother has a big crater on his nose where they removed a chunk of flesh that he "no longer needed." I still need all mine.

I drive through Burton, past the marina and turn onto Quartermaster Harbor. The road ends at the Isthmus of Maury. A left turn takes you back to Vashon and downtown. A right turn takes you to Maury.

PADDLES

My wife thinks that people from Maury Island believe that they are socially superior to the bumpkins from Vashon. Maybe they are right. There definitely *are* some doofuses on Vashon—but then they have those everywhere, don't they? Maury does have some first class homes. Gated entrances looking like they belong to some Hollywood star are tucked here and there.

We have had a few high rollers here. John Ratzenberger, who played Cliff Claven on "Cheers" had a home on Vashon for years, although I think he may have sold it. Other wealthy, but less famous, people have built homes here. Most of them get tired of it sooner or later. Living on an island is a hassle. Unless you have a helicopter (and there are a couple) you don't just head to Wall-Mart whenever you feel like it. You have to wait for the ferry.

I arrive at the Point Robinson park by 8:00. The gate is open from dawn to dusk only. They used to leave it open all the time, but it started to collect bored teens who left a lot of beer bottles and other problematic items around, so they changed the rules. I roll down the narrow, winding road, trying to stay on my side. The parking lot is empty. I get first choice. I pick the spot beside the Port-a-Potties. Very convenient.

Donning the Resistol-with-a-cork-cable-tied-to-it, I step out and survey the morning. I am disappointed to find that my rear line has come loose and the kayak has been in danger of falling off. I promise myself to secure it better next time and haul the 17-foot beast down onto the gravel. Rolling her up on his side with the cockpit toward me, I squat down and put both hands on the inside of the coaming. Like a lifter doing a clean and jerk, I explode with my legs and hoist the beast to neck level. Once there, I can stick my shoulder in the cockpit and support the coaming. I carry it like that down the short, flat track to the beach and set it down on the round stones a few feet from the water.

I return to the pickup for the paddles, spray skirt, PFD and plastic bag of goodies, then lock it up. Minutes later I am launching into blue water with white cirrus clouds above.

Point Robinson is a good place to fish for salmon and the first fishing boats arrived hours before me. I hear squeals of joy now and then from people who are sharing this year's bountiful catch.

I needn't have worried about the current. There isn't any. Out in the middle of the ship channel, just a mile east of the Point, there must be a northbound current of one or maybe almost two knots. But here by the shore it is calm in spite of the steep tidal gradient of over two feet per hour. I bring the boat to a dead stop with the paddle, watching to see that the bow wake goes calm. There is no motion at all relative to the land. A river rages a mile away, but I am in slack water. This will be an easy eight miles.

The Point is crowded with fishing boats, from the 12-foot aluminum variety to families in cruisers and runabouts. A few C-Dories and North River boats are there, too. High dollar fishing boats for the serious sportsman. These are rigged out with line holders and other equipment I don't even recognize. Every sport has gear heads.

I turn south, towards Piner Point five miles away. A quarter mile south of Point Robinson I am the only boat of any description. A breeze from the south carries away the sound of the fishermen. There is only me and the NC-17.

I pass a beautiful, and isolated new house on the beach. It is quite large—maybe ten thousand square feet. One of the gated entrances leads to this house. I'll never know which one. A man talks on a cell phone and watches me pass. We wave and smile.

Just south of the big house, there is a large hill covered with what people in Washington call "Madrona" trees. These are beautiful evergreen deciduous trees with peeling bark, and this is a large forest of them. The trees have a distinctive shape and the trunks always show a deep red color. The wood is mostly used here for firewood, and good firewood it is, at that. The BTU content is high because of the natural oil in the wood and the logs burn hot and long. But I am always saddened to see this rare wood sold so cheaply, because it makes beautiful furniture and art when it is put into the right hands.

I myself have made lovely objects from Madrona just by picking through a firewood pile. It is hard to dry, since it tends to cup, bow and twist. But if the miller cuts the pieces thick enough and just waits until it's done, he is rewarded with a beautiful dense stable hardwood that knows no equal in this country.

Canadians call the Madrona tree "Arbutus," using the Latin name: "Arbutus menziesii." The tree was originally named "Arbutus glauca" by Archibald Menzies, the surgeon of Vancouver's ship who first identified it, but the name was later changed in honor of his discovery. Californians, for reasons known only to themselves, call this wood "Madrone."

South of the Madrona forest, I pass the settlement of Gold Beach. It is a neat neighborhood of 1980s houses equally spaced and at just the right (and just the same) distance from the water. It looks like someone plucked a neighborhood from Issaquah and planted it smack on the beach without ruffling a bush. Nothing like this exists anywhere else on Vashon. Neat and clean as it is, some people have told me they think it's out of place.

For myself, though, I grant everyone the right to do what they want with their houses, and if the Gold Beachers are happy like that I wish them only the best. I felt terribly oppressed during that brief time when I lived in a house in California that was under the jurisdiction of a "neighborhood association." This is totalitarian collectivism at the neighborhood level and only those who are Nazis or Bolsheviks at heart could like it there. Paint your house pink, make it out of glass bottles, plant a cactus or a pine forest in your garden. Follow your own star and be happy!!!

Many years ago, when land was cheap on Maury Island, gravel prospectors working for an outfit that later became known as Glacier Inc. spotted a big deposit of glacial gravel (thus the name) in an otherwise challenging part of the island. They purchased a big tract of this land for a gravel mine. An islander bought an adjacent area and opened a local gravel company, "Vashon Sand and Gravel." For many years he sold sand and gravel to meet the construction and gardening needs of Vashon/Maury's growing population. Glacier constructed a dock and a conveyor system and began shipping gravel off the island. For reasons unknown to me at this writing, Glacier's operation stagnated and then fell into disuse.

In the 1990s SeaTac airport decided to build a third runway. Although it seems impossibly far away when you are in a kayak paddling the East Passage, in fact the distance is only seven or eight miles, and much of that can be traveled in a barge. Suddenly the gravel deposits on Maury became not only economically valuable but strategically important to the whole State of Washington.

That started a fist fight of Olympian proportions. Glacier and Vashon Sand and Gravel both sold out to Lone Star (no, they are not from Texas – they are from Japan). The Maury Islanders, worried about damage to their aquifer as well as the fact that gravel mining operations with their attendant loud clanking noises were planned for a 24/7 schedule, went to court. They went to their legislators, to the press, to the bumper sticker printers and to anyone else they thought might be able to help them win their battle.

The fight continues, but at this point it looks like the strategic concerns of the state, as well as the $50,000,000 (and growing) value of the land, trumps the concerns of the locals who are not able to actually *prove* that the aquifer will be damaged, and who after all should not have been surprised by the discovery of the gravel operation, it having been licensed since the 1950s, well before most of the houses were built. Probably some compromise will eventually be reached, but just now it is not clear what it will be.

On this beautiful August day, though, there is no clanking, only some rusty conveyor systems sticking out of the hillside and a rusty old ship, filled with metal scrap and painted with graffiti. Anchored next to the ship, just off the beach, a family in a sailboat readies their dinghy. Mom yells at the kids who are running on the beach. Dad yells at mom. The water around them boils with salmon, an endangered species.

I pass the neighborhood of Sandy Shores. It is an older development of more typical houses. The name is apt, since they do have a beautiful and quite long beach. A clump of neighbors chat as I paddle by. A toddler hugs her mother's leg.

I am getting ready for a break after almost six miles of paddling, so I decide to stop at Piner Point, which has an easy beach and is a nice place for a phone call or a picnic. When the tide is quite low, as it is this day, there is a big shelf of sand at the very point, making landing a kayak quite easy.

As I walk up the beach with my bottle of water and snacks, a horse clam squirts me just in the crotch. Since I am only wearing a boxer-style swim suite, the attack finds its mark. I would like to kill that clam, but that would mean digging, and I don't have a shovel, plus I have better things to do than seek revenge on a clam, so I decide to add mercy to my karmic scoreboard for today.

I eat some chips, almonds and a fruit bar, wishing I hadn't forgotten the thermos of tea. A quick call on the cell phone to report progress and I am itching to get back in the boat. Landing on Piner Point is usually pretty easy, but constant wake surf can make leaving a little harder. I push the boat into about a foot of water and struggle with the surges until I get all the parts in. A push with the paddle and I am a water creature again.

From Piner Point, the route passes across the mouth of Quartermaster Harbor. Here is about two miles of open water. The current is slow, since it is only about an hour to dead low tide, but on this beautiful Saturday there are lots of speeding boats filled with crazed salmon fishers and other boaters of unknown sobriety. Caveat kayaker.

I reach Neil Point at dead low tide. The point fathers a sand bar which extends out several hundred feet from the rocky bluffs. A fancy North River aluminum fishing boat has been trapped on the shoal, and the occupants nap inside, waiting for release. They don't look up as I paddle by.

Nearly to Tahlequah now, I see neighbors fishing on the beach.

Normally beach fishing is pointless, but during a big salmon run like this year, the endangered critter can be caught almost anyplace, since there is one about every five feet throughout the whole Puget Sound. Billions of endangered fish, and mighty tasty. They jump all around me as I get ready to land. One flops across the deck of the kayak, leaving a wet fish mark.

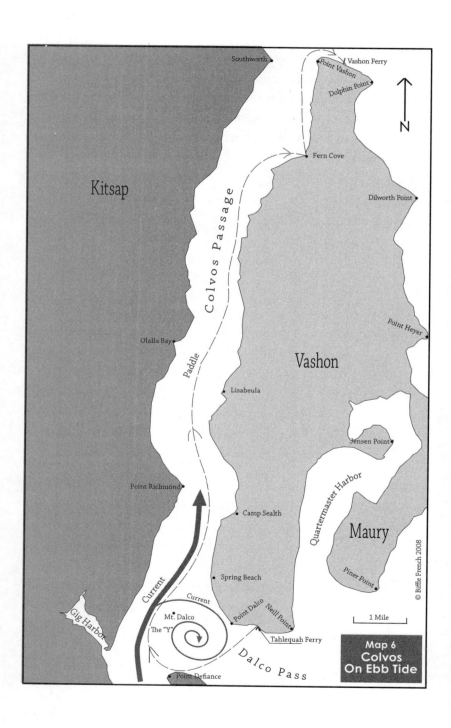

Colvos

I have waited for this day, and now it is here. This is the day of the August full moon, the best paddling day of August and possibly the best chance I will have for a Colvos passage trip. Full moon brings a spring tide, the big tide with the highest high and the lowest low. On the ebb of a spring tide is the time for a trip up the Colvos.

On the map, the distance from my beach to the north end boat ramp is about 12 miles, just following the shoreline and measuring with dividers. It gets longer as you measure more accurately, but that is just a map and not a paddle. When I use my GPS and measure the actual elapsed distance, it turns out to be closer to 18 miles, which is a good little excursion. Except for the part where you have to pass over the swirly rips to reach the northbound current, you could almost do the whole run with the boat facing south.

I have waited for this day, now it is here and I oversleep. If this is going to work at all, I have to get up at 4:30 am to make everything happen. But I don't. The alarm doesn't go off, and I open my eyes to see the clock showing 4:45, which is a bad sign. Normally, I would have woken up at 3:00 am and every fifteen minutes afterwards.

But recently Mike Cohen has been keeping me awake. Cohen is the developer of the Asarco property and he has offered to the City of Tacoma that he will redevelop Point Defiance Park in exchange for the right to build an amphitheater just across from my beautiful beach. I will have a front row seat. The problem is that I hate loud music and I'm not a big fan of crowds, especially when they clog up the ferry dock.

This is why I generally don't like other people. They are always screwing with me. Sartre was right: "Hell is other people." I never even heard of Mike Cohen until last week, and now he wants to run me out of my house. So I wake at midnight, mind racing. *Will I let him chase me out? Can I win the fight?* Later, I find some sleep. 4:30 comes and goes, I snore right through it.

I frantically make up the time by racing around pointlessly, not having a clue what I am supposed to do. I curse the stupid alarm clock and officially damn all alarm clocks to Hell. I find my keys, I find my shoes, I find my truck, I zoom out of the driveway. I have to catch a bus from the north end and I have to spot the truck in the car park first. Late comers don't get to park in the north end ferry parking, and the next bus is too late. I have to board this one or spend a worthless hour waiting in the ferry traffic, breathing fumes. Curse developers and city officials. May they all rot in Hell!

Only by speeding do I make it and I am the first passenger on the bus. I try not to speed any more, since that morning when my competitive instincts got the better of me. I was headed up Wax Orchard on the straightaway, when I saw headlights coming up fast behind me. It was still only twilight and I could not see the other car, but I knew what I needed to know.

"No sonofabitch has ever passed me on this road before and it's not going to happen today", I said out loud, proving again that I am not rational. I often say things out loud when I am alone, and sometimes when I am not, a habit that others find disturbing. People from the Other Side do that, but I am not one them. No, really, I'm not.

While at IBM, I once made a suggestion that we charitably collect old, dead Bluetooth headsets and give them to the crazies so they would fit in to society. If you say things out loud while wearing a headset, people think you are just like them. It would be a public service.

As the headlights got closer I had to speed up a bit to keep him behind me, where he rightly deserved to be. Tires squealed around corners, I was putting the old truck through all the gears. Still he came and still I tried to keep ahead.

It was only as the sun was a bit higher that I got a look at the side of his Cherokee as I rounded a corner before he did. It had a sheriff's star on it. I was prey.

The bus pulls out of the ferry dock at 5:15 and begins to collect other passengers right away. I chat them up about the amphitheater, but their reaction is muted. One woman who apparently sees the world in different terms than I do says "Don't you like music?"

"I like Chopin, but not at 2:00 am." Her vacant stare shows too clearly the gulf between us.

At home I quickly change into trunks and a long-sleeved T-shirt. I load my bag of food and water, make a thermos of hot tea, and grab a Polartec jacket in case I fall in and need to get warm again. I stuff all that into the rear compartment, load up the paddles, bilge pump, rescue bag, skirt and PFD. Squatting down like an Olympic wrestler, I put my hands into the cockpit and e*xplode.*

But with all that junk inside, the boat is much heavier than I expect, and my exploding just causes me to slip and stumble. The kayak stays pretty much where it was, on the deck. Finally I am able to get the bow up, then I wrestle up the heavy stern. I am wobbly with all that load so high up, but at least I don't have to make two trips to the beach.

In the water we are graceful again and I paddle out behind the ferry, aiming for Point Defiance and the northbound current. I have always wondered why the fish like to hang about near Point Dalco or Point Defiance, so I decide to ask a fisherman for his opinion. I see a man my age or a little older, rather heavy and with a stubble on his face. He looks at me, so I think we can speak. I smile and nod. He looks away. Well, it is Washington.

In these waters today, though, fishermen are as plentiful as fish. Even more so, in fact: nobody is getting anything. I catch the eye of another fisherman, a man with a nice, new-looking aluminum rig. His fishing rod is some kind of fixed machine that sticks out the side of his fancy boat. "Mornin'", I say.

"Morning", he responds, thinking I will now leave him the hell alone.

"Can I ask you a question?" I know he doesn't have any other particular plans right then and he's sure not catching any fish.

"Sure"

"Why do you think the fish like to be here or at Dalco and no place else?"

"Well, it's just a preference, I guess. They seem to congregate here on the Point Defiance side when the tide's going out and over there on the Dalco side when it's coming in. I'm not catching any either place today, though."

"Oh?"

My friend David, a marine biologist, says that the points funnel the fish to one place. They don't have any better route to where they're going. But I do like the preference explanation a lot, too.

Paddling past the northernmost of today's few fishing boats, I am in the open part of the Y and headed for the northbound current. I feel a freedom here, a lack of the oppression of nearby land. Every direction is open, all things are possible.

Seals are always everywhere in the Y, searching for salmon and sometimes for sex, like horny teenagers. I see their heads everywhere, sometimes five or six at a time, very close to where I am. They stay above and rest or even sleep for a few minutes here in the Y.

A big male spots me from fifty yards away and submerges quickly. He makes a loud, purposeful splash as he goes under, warning his mate who is sleeping nearby. She awakens, sees the danger and joins him under the water. Seal fear kayakers like the Shih Tzu fear deer. It is inborn.

Native hunters survived on seal for thousands of years farther north. The Eskimo took seals for food, clothing, and kayak parts. Driftwood frames were covered with animal skins, seal or sometimes caribou. The hides were held in place with seal sinew or seal gut.

Eskimo hunters made floats from inflated seal bladders, and used them for hunting everything from seals to whales. When an animal was harpooned, the detachable barb was tied to a line that connected to an inflated seal bladder. The impaled animal had to fight the buoyancy of the bladder to dive, and would quickly exhaust itself. The bladder float remained on top of the water, giving the hunters a marker and a leash so they could haul in their prey and administer the kill when the time came.

Some Eskimos believe that seals volunteer for death to help out the hunters, and that the soul of a seal remains with its bladder until it is reborn upon being returned to the sea. Seals know that this all is just a bunch of self-serving Eskimo bullshit, of course, and refuse to be taken in by it. Nowadays, whenever a seal sees a paddler he shudders as he imagines an afterlife where he is trapped in his own bladder, festooning the side of a kayak. If a seal had knees, they would grow weak at the thought. Seals can never be friends with kayakers—they want to keep their bladders on the *in*side.

That said, I have had seals stalk *me* out in the Y. I feel their eyes on my back, or hear them snorting. When I turn around there may be three or four of them watching me from fifty feet away or even closer, black eyes open wide. Sometimes they challenge me to a staring contest, other times the leader splashes a warning when he knows he is caught, and they all dive at once. What are they thinking?

Now I am in the strong northbound current. The south Sound empties through the Narrows and on the ebb of a spring tide, like today, there is a nozzle effect. Planetary volumes of water come vomiting out through the narrow gorge. The water speeds up and is forced straight north, through the Colvos. I'm in the core now, and I am going for a ride.

The Colvos and the Y are completely different worlds. Where the Y seems endless and open, the Colvos Passage is narrow, averaging about a mile in width for its full length. Looking at it on a map it is clear that Vashon was once married to Kitsap. They divorced long ago, and now Vashon lives alone.

Where the Y is loud with boat noises, train noises and the constant hum of distant freeways, the Colvos is quiet. There is such a hush here that even a flock of geese, honking encouragement to each other as they fly, seems loudly out of place. When they land and stop their honking the silence is delicious.

I hear a small plane overhead, and looking up I see a V-tail Bonanza traveling north along the Colvos, following my route, but above me at about a thousand feet. These are old planes, yet very fast, even compared to many newer aircraft, but they do bite. The old V-tails have a problem with overspeed: if the pilot lets the airspeed build too high in a dive, the tail structure does not have the strength to raise the nose again and it fails by cracking. So the dive steepens, and the plane is lost. It usually breaks up in flight—the G forces pull off the wings as it tumbles with no elevator or rudder. That used to happen a lot before people figured out why—a good friend lost some family members that way back in the sixties. Even so, I always wanted one. What a beautiful ride they are! But do watch your airspeed.

When the Bonanza is past, it is quiet again. I can hear someone pounding nails with a hammer, far away on the Kitsap side. The Vashon shore is much less populated, and there is no more lovely setting than the west side of Vashon. To paddle the Colvos is to see a rare beauty.

As I approach Lisabeula I see a giant articulated tug-barge coming straight toward me from about a mile north. The turquoise and white tower on the tug is directly in the middle of the barge from my point of view. If we keep this up I will be an ex-kayaker very soon. It seems that he is turning more toward me as I try to escape to the east, toward Vashon. There is a nervous moment as I start to paddle at hull speed, aiming directly at the Vashon shore. Finally, I see him bring the barge around to his starboard, so I am safe. I realize he was probably avoiding a shoal. Southbound tugs need to stay near the shore to avoid the strongest currents, and those are usually in the center of the passage. The tide is going out fast now, though, and where there are shoals he has to miss them, even if it means aiming directly at kayakers.

There is an underwater cable that passes between Lisabeula and Olalla Bay on the Kitsap side. It was there, at Olalla Bay, that Lt. Puget saw the Indians run away and abandon their canoe, fearful of the armed intruders in their bigger boats. It was there, in Olalla Bay, that he saw high tide marks at 14 feet above his current level, and realized the power of the coming tidal flood. That is where he left some peace offerings, in the abandoned canoe. Right there, where now there is an ugly cable, a bridge and a few houses, there were frightened Indians on that day, escaping softly into the woods to avoid the foreigners, watching them from the forest, and later finding strange beads and medals when they reclaimed their beloved dugout. To the aboriginal mariner, a boat is life.

On the Vashon side north of where the Indians saw Lt. Puget there is a beautiful beach called Fern Cove. I stop there for a rest. Eel grass waves on the sandy bottom and makes it hard to judge the depth. I pull the boat in until I strike sand, then I get out, and lifting it by the coaming I place it gently on the beach.

This is a great moment for some tea and guacamole chips, so I dig in. I didn't feel hungry before, now I do. The warm tea is delicious, but I clumsily slop it all over everything and pour plenty into the open hatch. I am too happy to curse, however, so I forgive myself and sponge up the mess.

Fern Cove meets the Colvos with a sandy beach, the product of a stream flowing down the hillside above. Mountain streams like the one feeding the Fern Cove beach carry a lot of silt, and that creates a sandy delta where nature otherwise would have left only barnacle-covered stones.

Above the sandy area there is a rocky section strewn with boulders that also has a couple of giant fallen tree trunks lying parallel to the beach. Tree trunks like these line beaches all over the Pacific Northwest, and they are very dangerous. They look immobile as they lie there on the stones, tons of wood that can't be moved. But when the tide comes in closer they can float like corks if a big wave or wake washes under them, and they will crush anyone unlucky enough to be standing in the path.

Standing in the shadows of tall trees and looking at the NC-17 on the quickly-growing beach, I see the view down the blue Colvos. A fancy red and white cruising boat, made to resemble an old tug, parades gently northward up the center of the passage. He takes the same advantage I did of the current. There are few boats here, in spite of the beautiful day, and he is one of only three I see while I rest. He's half a mile away so he likely does not notice me taking my tea and eating my chips on the beautiful, secluded beach.

A belted kingfisher chatters in the trees above, although I don't see him. The beautiful birds nest in tunnels in the soft bluffs that they team dig using their bills. The pair take turns—one digging while its mate rapidly kicks the loosened dirt out the tunnel opening, raising a gritty spray. They make their tunnels several feet long and carve out a special nesting chamber at the back where they can safely raise their chicks in the darkness.

I suddenly become concerned that I will have to move the heavy kayak a long way to get back in the water. The beach is growing quickly as the tide continues to ebb. I button everything up and launch again hastily. My friend, the north current, pushes me on.

I find the sweet spot at the flow center again and drive along like a bicyclist on the interstate, imagining I am the only one who is coming today. A loud noise behind me shakes me out of my reverie, it is the tinny sound of an amplified voice, the voice of the announcer on a big Argosy cruise boat that is loaded with thirteen-year-old kids. I am in his way and he's not giving me an inch.

"Look kids, a kayak", the announcer says, desperate for anything to keep their attention. A couple of the kids, who are dancing around with their hands in the air start to wave at me, and I wave back, but I am not happy about the situation.

"Look kids, a kayak", he says again, and this time even more of them frantically gesture.

"Look asshole, a wake", I say, seeing the three-foot-tall, curling, swirling wake that the party boat trails. "This is going to be interesting", I say out loud, thinking that "interesting" does not really cover it.

The boat passes, the kids wave, I paddle, then the wake "takes me from behind", if you know what I mean, and I think you do. The wakes from many boats are somewhat coherent and generate a diminishing series of long, parallel waves, but not this one. It has what really amounts to two wakes, angled against each other to create a kind of liquid moiré.

Parallel wakes are unsettling enough, although their actual arrival is always anticlimactic. This one is like skiing steep chopped-up moguls. The boat rises, dips, rises and plops down when the wave just disappears in a huge trough. I get in trail with the boat, so I can just cross all the wake elements at once and be done with it. Here, directly behind, it leaves gentle rollers. Less obnoxious than the wake to be sure, but I was much happier before he came.

The announcer's voice is still audible for a while. A young man trying to wow much younger teens. I am glad when it is out of range. The paddle is good again. The rollers have flattened out and the water is perfect.

As the Argosy boat dwindles into the distance I see the top of Mount Baker come into view directly ahead. I skied there a few times about fifteen years ago and every time I see it the memories return. It is still completely snow covered, at least as seen from sea level in the Colvos. The late summer haze blurs it a bit, but for an object almost 100 miles away, it is still very impressive.

Baker is under 11,000 feet tall, so it is no match for Rainier, but it is still a huge pile of rock, an active volcano and part of the chain that is sometimes called the Pacific "Ring of Fire."

Suddenly I see the Southworth ferry poking out behind the bend. The paddle is almost over and there's no stopping it. As I reach the northern extremity of the Colvos and round the bend I see the Vashon ferry dock ahead. This is civilization again with lots of houses and so many motor sounds I can not associate each sound with a particular object. There are ferries, power boats, a couple airplanes, lawn mowers, weedeaters and who knows what else. It comes on you suddenly, like the Argosy, because it is so easy to get lulled into the hypnotic calm of the passage. I feel like I've changed centuries.

The current has forsaken me now as well. I look down at the kelp as I cross into the shallow water and see that the leaves are flowing toward me – the current is fighting me and it is fairly powerful. I struggle to get past the last half mile to the boat ramp. The battle against the current is surprising after seventeen miles with hardly any struggle at all. I was not looking for it and my legs are pretty worn out by now, so this little bit of uphill paddling, coming just at the end, is very demanding.

Finally, I reach the beach, on the west side, and struggle once again to load my extra-heavy kayak on my shoulder. When I can manage I walk under the pilings and place the boat on the rocks.

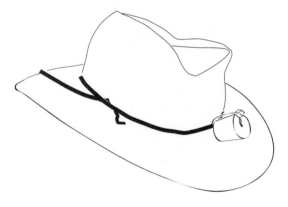

A woman in her sixties is walking the beach nearby. She is wearing a long print dress and has on orange sunglasses with orange lenses. "This will be interesting", I think to myself. When she comes into range I speak.

"Hi there", I say, hoping she won't notice that I am wearing a sweaty Resistol with a cork cable-tied to it.

"Well hi there" she drawls in what I take to be a Georgia accent.

"Is that Georgia I hear?"

"I'm from South Belleview" she jokes, putting diphthongs where no Washingtonian would dare.

I tell her I'm from Texas and she says I should use the Texas accent more. She likes to hear it. Then she admits she's from Mississippi, a state where I lived for a year while I was in Air Force Undergraduate Pilot Training. Suddenly we are lifelong friends. Southerners know it's only pretend, of course, but we think it brightens up the world when strangers can smile and tell personal things. Chinese would never consider it, but once you are both from Mississippi, there is nothing you can not share.

"I got the brain cancer, you know", she admits, "so we moved over here where it's a little easier life than Belleview. I'm supposed to be dead now, but I think I'm gonna be good for a while yet. I love it here on Vashon...Well, nice to see you." She climbs the barnacle-covered ramp and is gone.

I trot up the hill to the parking lot, start the truck and drive back down to "La Playa" and the boat ramp. I carry the NC-17 up the ramp, load her onto the kayak carrier and tied her down. Then I back into a parking stall, walk inside and eat one of the best Chile Relleno dinners I've had in my life.

Hunger is the best sauce, and life does not get any better than this. "I should do it again tomorrow", I think, but then I realize that my legs may need a day to recover. Eighteen miles is a long paddle for an old man, even with the current.

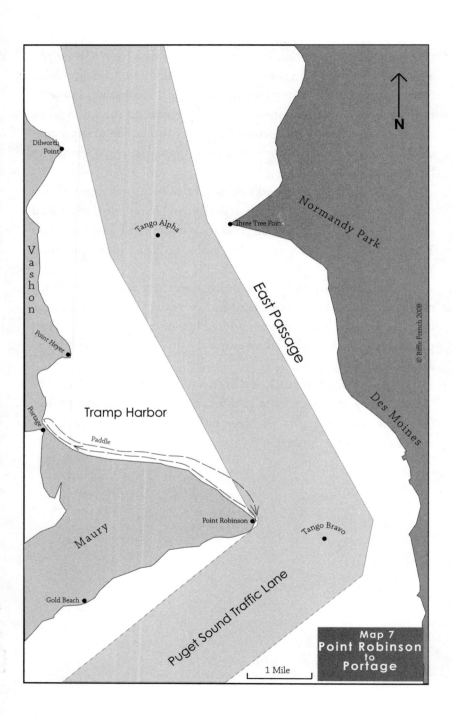

Point Robinson to Portage

It is September and the days are getting shorter much too fast for me. These are the perfect waning days of summer, soft and warm days, perfect for paddling. My circuit of the island is almost complete already, only a couple more short paddles to finish it.

Today I decide to make the short paddle from Point Robinson to the fishing pier at Tramp Harbor, an eight mile round trip. It is the 20th day of the moon, five days after full and I go in the morning, on the ebb, as the tide drops below about 9 feet.

The lighthouse at Point Robinson always gets my notice. These days it is ringed with weather sensors, ship radar and communication towers, but it is still there, well kept, and even with all our modern paraphernalia around it you can still see it for itself. It is a small building and the light tower is not very tall at all, but it has beautiful red, green and white color and a real architectural charm that add a lot to an already beautiful setting.

To the southeast, across the rising land of Federal Way, stands Mt. Rainier, almost invisible in the haze and blinding sunlight. The Mountain will be easier to see later, when the sun is in the west, now it is almost just a promise.

I launch near the white clapboard caretaker's house and paddle quickly around the Point, heading west. This rocky beach is a great launch site, and on a smooth day like today, with no wind at all and no wakes it is dreamily perfect. The north side of Maury Island can be quite rough during a storm, but today it is glassy.

In the first half mile there is only one house on the beach, and from here Maury Island looks much like it must have before Vancouver's crew gave the Indians their first trinkets.

Of course, there were whites in the Pacific Northwest before Vancouver—his fame was the achievement of his charts. British, Russians and Spaniards had sailed the coast for years, and Spain at one time claimed the entire Pacific coast. The Spaniards had more than they could handle in California, and Mexico, though, and the Russians were busy trapping furs in Alaska. Indians had some trade with both before Vancouver came, although maybe Vashon Indians had never seen whites before. Still, they probably did know such warlike people existed, if only from rumor. Indians called them "Drifting White People."

It was only a few years before Vancouver, on the 14th of July, 1775 that seven members of the crew of a Spanish schooner, the Sonora were attacked as they landed in a longboat to collect water from the Quinault river. Wielding bows and arrows as well as spears, as many as 200 Quinault Indians suddenly surrounded the unsuspecting Spaniards. They wanted metal, and the unlucky visitors had plenty.

In the 17 years after that attack, the Salish-speaking Quinaults likely bragged to everyone they met about their great victory over the Spaniards, who were forced to flee in the undermanned Sonora after destroying an attacking Quinault canoe with a swivel cannon.

So the Indians of Vashon, who may never have seen a white man before Vancouver's crew arrived, probably knew at least something about them. They knew that they were men, and so could be killed, and also that they had terrible fire weapons capable of destroying a canoe at a distance. They knew that they came in sailing ships and had metal. They knew that the price of metal was sometimes blood.

As I paddle the easy north shore of Maury Island I imagine those gentle people, living in the gentle rain forest, plotting the murder of some thirsty Spaniards, watching the ship move up the coast with its sails, towing the long boats. How powerful they must have felt, rushing from the forest in their hundreds, impaling the unwary Europeans with arrow and spear, waving their captured muskets, balls, helmets, swords and breastplates. A bonanza of metal, bought with foreigner's blood and some of their own.

Now I paddle northwest and I reach the houses along Luana Beach Rd. There are quite a few of them lining the beach. Some look like they may have been fishing shacks at one time, remodeled and rebuilt for sixty years or more. Modern here and ancient there. It looks a lovely place to live, though, and there are people about on their low bank yards close to the water.

I see an elderly man, probably in his late seventies, shoveling concrete into a bulkhead repair.

"Mornin'," I say.

He looks up and focuses his eyes on me. "Mornin'."

"Don't worry, I'm not from King County." He smiles, I wave and paddle on.

On a day like today, kayaking is almost like snorkeling. Here in the clear shallows of Tramp Harbor I am in water that looks like air. I am floating. There is no current and there are no waves or even wakes, not so much as a roller to give any texture or substance to the surface. Only my waterbug's bow wave shows me where the water is, otherwise it would disappear.

The light is perfect with the sun behind me, and the bottom shows completely in full daylight. The eelgrass waves are frozen like a ladies permanent curl from the lack of current and schools of bait fish dart about. What can they be searching for, or escaping from? Maybe they just enjoy the darting – if I could dart like that, I'd do it all the time.

I pass a big house, what we used to call a "mansion" when I was a kid. This one has a barrel vault and four large columns on the front. There are lots of windows looking out across the immaculate lawn, and a gardener tends the bushes. I wonder who lives there.

Another house catches my eye, near the end of houses. It has a beautiful northwest Indian totem pole sticking up in the yard. It is one of the best I've ever seen, but it is not painted as they usually are, so it must have been there for some time. Indians made totem poles from soft cedar for a centuries, but the production was small, owing to the lack of metal tools. Once they were able to trade fur for iron or steel, they could make adzes and axes, useful for carving big totems. After Salish-speaking people had plenty of metal tools, totems appeared everywhere, the fortuitous confluence of Indian art and European mining and manufacture.

After Luana Beach, there is a long section, maybe a mile, where there are no houses on the beach at all, only above, on steep bluffs. That section goes all the way to Portage, and today there is not a soul there but me, just offshore in my kayak.

The bluff in one area has slumped away and you can see the vertical face. Bluffs like this are unstable and more can slough away any time. It is not safe to stand there. There are places in Seattle where expensive houses that were built at the tops of high bluffs have come sliding down and now lay all catawampus on the beach, far below where guests used to sit in the hot tub, drink wine, and look at the city lights on a drizzly winter evening. I wonder if such a house sits above this bluff, out of sight and in dreadful danger.

Passing the gray sandy wall of the eroding bluff I see a flowery anemone in the shallow water. It is pure white and its segments make it look like an albino ice plant. I've seen lots of anemones on Vashon, but never one like this.

A caterpillar floats on the water surface, lying on his side. I suppose he must have fallen from one of the trees that shelter and hide the bluffs. Suddenly I see another one, peas in a pod. These fat little fellows are bright white, fuzzy and with red stripes. What a photo opportunity, but I don't have my camera.

There is a store at Portage, where you can buy snacks and things, but I have never been in it, so I can't really tell its story well. What I do know is this: out in the front of that store there are some ancient rusty exercise bikes where people sometimes sit on the low bluff overlooking the beach and sweat and grunt through a spin class in the weeds, just next to the road. This is something that would never happen in California, it is too public and just not tony.

As I get near to Portage, imagining that I am with lifelong friends, hiding in the bushes while waiting to ambush Spaniards, there is the loud sound of a bright red ambulance speeding south on Dockton Road. Someone has had a heart attack or fallen off a ladder. Maybe some kayaker has rolled over and can't get up. The Big Red Ambulance is off to save the day. Loudly.

I had a friend in Austin who sold ambulances in the mid 70's. He was quite successful, although he later went to prison for a long time because he thought he could make even *more* money selling dope. We used to have great fun back then, turning on the lights and siren, driving like hell through the streets with absolute impunity, getting high. The best fun was playing doctor on a gurney in the back with our dates. Whenever I see a Big Red Ambulance zooming along, lights flashing, siren blaring, I always wonder who's really in there and where they are really going.

When I get to Portage I decide I've had enough, even though I planned to go all the way to the fishing pier, still half a mile away. It's hot and airless now in that part of Tramp Harbor and I'd rather stay near the cool bluffs. I begin to feel a paranoid fear that a fast-moving car, driven by careless teens, might run off Dockton Road and flatten me like a tortilla here in the shallow water, so I turn the boat around and head back toward Point Robinson.

Nothing is the same the second time, nothing in the universe. The first kiss, a new paddle are qualitatively different than the second kiss or the return trip. You have found it, and now there is nothing else to seek. Now it is just turning the crank, letting the mind wander, pushing the boat along.

I decide to up the pace. The heart starts to beat faster and my muscles warm a bit to their task. There is a current flowing, and it is hard in my face. I know everything now—it becomes just another workout. I must get home to write this book.

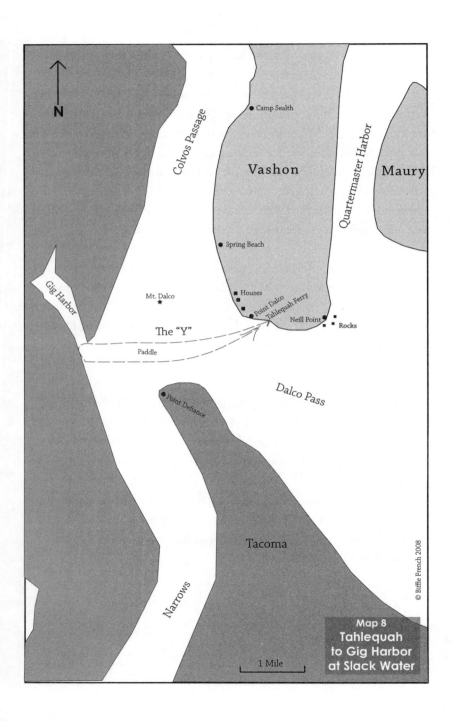

Tahlequah to Gig Harbor

A good open-water paddle is from Tahlequah to Gig Harbor and back. It is about seven miles, round trip, and most of it is a mile or more from land. It is a paddle that has lots of faces, depending on the weather and on the tides.

It's early October this day. I know that the change is coming, and soon, but today it's still pleasant. It's gray and cloudy, but not cold yet, and there is no wind or rain. I picked a neap tide day, and left before the bottom of the ebb. The current flowing into the Narrows can be quite strong during the flood. The best time to cross the Y is at slack water.

The cormorants have been here for a while now. The first ones arrived in August. I hated to see them come, because I knew they'd bring the fall, and here it is. But there is no holding them back. They line the ruin of the old ferry dock, a remnant of the Mosquito Fleet, their charcoal-gray wings held up to dry, their fat bellies full of fish.

Cormorants are easy to spot from a distance because of the characteristic way they have of drying their wings when they rest. Although they are water birds, their feathers are not waterproof, so they have to dry them. These dark, long-necked birds range the world, always living in coastal areas.

In Tierra Del Fuego, at the southern tip of Argentina, where the Cape Horn eats ships with its fifty-foot waves and hundred mile an hour williwaws, the Fuegians, naked nomadic mariners who kept fires in their canoes, ate the greasy birds. Europeans never managed to develop a taste for cormorants, and now the Fuegians are all gone, so nobody eats them anymore.

I paddle past the dock, alone. In summer these waters are full of fishermen with their aluminum or glass boats. They motor about, avoiding each other. They cast their lines and haul in big, thrashing salmon. They talk to each other across the water and shout with joy when a prize catch breaks the water. They bring the smell of gasoline. A kayak is in their way.

The feeling of being alone on the water on a day like this is a religious pleasure. Other people frequently piss me off and out here they generally can't do it. Out here there's just my boat, my body and the rollers.

Dalco Pass is the name of the area between Tahlequah and Point Defiance. Point Dalco lies to the northwest. Dalco Pass meets the Narrows to the south and Colvos Passage to the north making an upside-down 'Y'.

The point at Point Defiance aims directly at Gig Harbor, but you can't see the actual harbor from Dalco Pass. In fact, it is not visible at all from a kayak until you are almost at the entrance. As I pass across the center of the Y, I feel a serene calm. Everywhere is the Sound, it is a mile to land in any direction.

Crossing the Y I look south at the two narrows bridges. During World War II, my Dad was a new second lieutenant in the U.S. Army Artillery when he passed through here on a troop ship. I have a letter he wrote to my grandmother on that trip. In it he drew a sketch of the first Tacoma Narrows Bridge, "Galloping Gertie." By that time, the bridge had already failed, a victim of misunderstood engineering. My Dad's sketch shows the roadbed hanging from the supports.

The original designers did not understand resonance very well and had only a limited ability to model it. The basic differential equations were known, but to create a series, each parameter had to be altered and each new solution calculated with a slide rule. Nowadays, the differential equations needed to test a system like this are packaged in modeling software that is available to any engineer, but back then, back before Galloping Gertie the stakes were not so clear.

So the bridge failed. And it hung there, flaccid as an old man, for all the years of the world war.

I enter the little cove that announces Gig Harbor, looking for the entrance. Even on a low-traffic day like this, it is too busy in there for a kayak, so I just peer in from the canal. This sheltered harbor, wall-to-wall with marinas, is a place for power boats and a kayak needs a good reason to enter.

So I turn the boat around and point the bow home. It has been a good paddle with a favorable current and no wind, but now slack water has passed and the flood has started. I will have to slog back uphill.

I cross the mouth of the Narrows at cruising speed, wanting to clear the area before the current builds. Back in the Y, I am fighting a small, but building current. I made almost five miles per hour coming over, my best cruising speed, now I am making about three. Five feels fast and three feels like a crawl. You would not think that such a small difference would matter much – only two miles per hour – but as a percentage of my speed it is huge, and I certainly can feel it.

As I cross the Y, I see an enormous barge headed my way. I don't know his speed, but he looks slow enough to avoid. The tug is a type called ATB – articulated tug-barge. The barge and tug are a system. The tug fits into a large notch at the rear of the barge. It has massive connecting bars that mate into sockets on the barge. Hydraulic rams push the bars home into the sockets.

Barges like this are better for calm seas, since they can start to buck if waves are too heavy. They roll with the barge, but they can pitch independently. When the barge is two hundred feet behind, connected by a chain, there is a little more leeway for nature to act up.

Sometimes I see immense flat barges full of tree trunks with the bark still on. These scows often carry a giant power hoe to move the load. The trees are milled into lumber, and the big pile of sawdust is hauled to the paper mill in Tacoma on a later trip.

This barge is black and rusty, as they all are. The blue and white tug is built with a tall bridge tower so the operator can keep a lookout over the top. I can see the cabin as I cross her path, but she is too far away for me to get a view of the operator up in the bridge. I can't see what the barge is loaded with either, so it may be an empty. I can see that she is going to pass well clear, but I know that I am trespassing. This is a heavy traffic lane and I am a bicycle on the freeway again. A one-speed with pedal brakes.

Vashon is ahead now. I can see the yellow house on Point Dalco up ahead. A kayaker has his best chance along the beach whenever the current is strong like this. Friction from the land mass slows the current and lessens the struggle. I head for the shoreline and paddle close and parallel to it.

Just past the ferry dock I pass a lady who looks to be maybe sixty-five years old or so. She is looking at stones on the beach, trying to find a special one. She sees me paddle by and looks up. There is something strange and unexpected in her glance.

She is strolling toward my landing spot and I feel like talking, so I take my time getting the kayak out and wait for her to arrive.

"Hi there," I say, "looking for rocks?"

"Yes, I like these gray ones." She shows me a hardened lump of Vashon clay that has been shaped into a smooth sculpture by the action of the water.

Clay like this forms much of the island and the sea floor. It is usually covered by gravel or stones, sometimes by sand. But it is always there, and sometimes it comes to the surface. At low tide it hardens a bit in the sun, but it has no resistance to abrasion and so it forms these pleasing, smooth shapes.

For many years this smooth Vashon clay was used to make bricks, and worn red bricks, rounded from years of kicking around the sea floor, constantly wash up on the beach.

"I saw you kayaking just now, as I was walking up the beach."

"Yeah, I just came from over there: Gig Harbor."

"Aren't you afraid?"

I was taken back a bit by the direct question. Afraid?

"Well, I know how to self rescue. I have my rescue gear with me. I'll be OK."

"Oh." She seemed unconvinced.

"I've never seen you before. Do you live here on the beach?," I asked.

"Well, we have an old beach house here. It belonged to my Dad. But I live in Seattle. I've come to Vashon all my life, though. I had four sons and we all used to kayak here all the time. I used to be a big kayaker. Not anymore though. Not for about five years."

"Where is your house?"

"Just down there. You passed it when you paddled by."

"So...what do you do in Seattle?"

"I'm an artist. I make pretty things. Objets d'art."

"Gee, that's great. An artist. I'm kind of an artist myself. I like to make things, too. I make furniture. Right now I'm making Chinese chairs. I'll show them to you sometime if you're interested."

"I'd like that...sometime. Yes, that would be interesting. I used to kayak, you know. My sons were raised with kayaks. But then one of them drowned. I don't do it anymore."

She got a look on her face that I'd seen before. She was remembering the phone call. "...about your son..."

"Drowned? How old was he? How long ago?"

"He was forty. It was at Lake Union. It was about five years ago."

"What happened? I mean how did..."

"They don't know. Nobody knows. He was kayaking, and they found him later. Now I don't kayak anymore."

"I'm so...sorry."

"Well, nothing to do about it now. Things happen. That's a very pretty boat you have. Just be careful."

"Yes, I will."

"Well I've got to go pick up rocks. Nice meeting you."

"Yeah, you too."

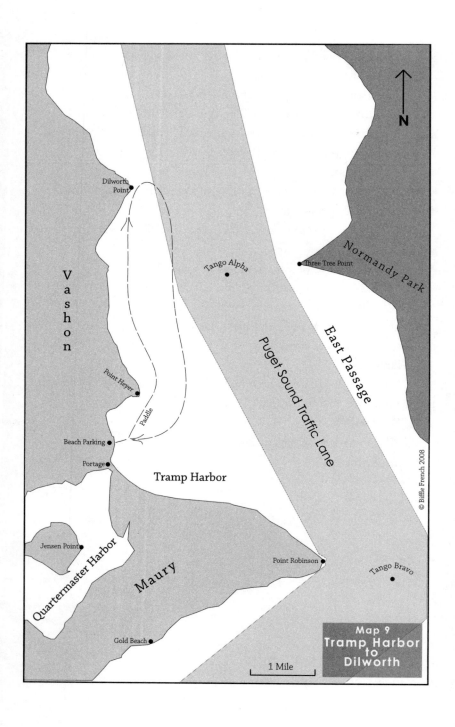

Tramp Harbor to Dilworth Point

It is American Labor Day – the one in September, not the Communist one on May 1st. Today is my last paddle but one for this book. I will travel from Tramp Harbor Beach to Dilworth Point and back. Today, like every Labor Day for the last 20 years, is perfect. A few high clouds gentle the sun and there is no wind at all. The careful eye sees a haze just above the water, forming well off in the distance.

I ready the craft on the beach as I have so many times, and apologize to her for her many battle scars. I am guilty of all of them. I try to be careful but I am clumsy, while she is long, awkward, and rather heavy.

Big clumps of green algae sully the water just at the shoreline. It is clingy and troublesome as it covers my booties and wraps around the paddle. I try to shake it off as I enter the cockpit, but in the end I have to remove each colony by hand. It is diaphanous and weak, only one or two cells layers thick, so it pulls apart, then it sticks to the boot and my hand. It is very messy, and it takes me a while to get rid of it.

Finally free of the accursed chlorophyta I start to paddle northeast to round Point Heyer. On this cool, beautiful, late summer morning there is only one person walking on the sandy beach, where often there are crowds —I have picked the perfect day.

Aside from the big piles of green algae sloshing around near the beach, Tramp Harbor is perfectly clear again today. I can easily see the sandy bottom in water more than ten feet deep. At my beach there is a constant arrival of flotsam, including empty beer bottles and broken boat parts—even ancient bricks wash up. But here the bottom is perfectly clean, and seeing that makes me unexpectedly happy.

For someone who is used to paddling around Tahlequah, where even a neap tide is a show of force and drama, Tramp Harbor is an amazing display of Nature's benign tranquility. I've never been here in a storm, but today at least, I am seeing a lovely girl with all her makeup on just right and a gentle smile on her sweet face.

Around Point Heyer you can clearly see the tall bluffs at Dilworth

Point, about three miles north. It looks close, but I know it will likely take me almost an hour to get there. The shortest path is not the most interesting one.

As I paddle along the shore there seems to be no current at all, and I notice that I am making 5 mph, a really good speed. I feel strong and excited today, Mr. Pigafetta is almost home.

I'm surprised that there are no seals surfacing in this part of the East Passage. There are no fishermen either. Nor are there any sailboats or other kayakers. In fact there is nobody at all. In two miles of water there is only me and my scarred-up lime-green kayak on this beautiful American Labor Day morning. Just me and the blue sky and the clear, calm, blue water.

As I paddle by the neighborhoods on the shore, I begin to see that this is the tony part of the island. Most of the houses have new paint and well-kept gardens. None are like the house next to mine, with its briar patch of fifteen-foot high blackberries climbing up the deck into the old hot tub and scratching at the back door. All of these houses show the signs of loving hands and money.

North from the Klahanie neighborhood there is a house, an estate, rather, that looks like it must be worth ten to twenty million. Enormous, beautifully designed and perfectly maintained, it looks almost like a Disneyland castle with its round tower and grassy lawn. It is exactly where I'd like to be invited to tea.

This eastern shore has houses everywhere, but they are helter-skelter, not lined up like soldiers on parade. Here one peeks from the trees, there one stares over the bluff. Unlike nearby Chautauqua and Klahanie, there is no sense of traveling through a neighborhood. Instead, there is a definite feeling of a few lucky souls living on a wild beach. The paddler feels real visual pleasure, looking from the water, seeing tall green trees on the graveled shore.

At Dilworth Point, I am back in the suburbs – here the houses are packed together into a crowd again. Still, it looks a good place to be, and certainly no more crowded that our little neighborhood. There is a huge, white, fiberglass catamaran moored at the point, probably belonging to one of the residents. I have seen this boat motor by my house many times, and now I wonder if this is where the owner lives.

At Dilworth I have reached my destination for today, so I swing around and *wham!!* it hits me: I have been going the wrong direction. Headed south now, I am looking directly at the Mountain, and seeing it from a direction and in a setting that is absolutely magnificent. Now that I can see past Point Robinson, I am peering down the full length of the East Passage and there is Mt. Rainier, fifty miles away through clear skies and with no obstructions. He looks like a mythical object – a mirage maybe, placed just so for my entertainment and seemingly so clear and close I can almost touch him. The blue water below with its inexplicable purple hues, the blue sky above with patches of high, white cloud, and there in the center, the Mountain – white and blue, massive and exhilarating.

The last eruption of Mt. Rainier was in 1840, well after the first white settlers arrived, and so it is well documented. But that was a small eruption, just a warning, and anyway the population around the volcano was small then. Large eruptions of Rainier occur regularly, though, with the last happening maybe 1,000 years ago or so. We are likely due again. According to the U.S. Geological Survey:

> "Mount Rainier has been the source of numerous lahars (volcanic debris flows) that buried now densely-populated areas as far as 100 km (62 miles) from the volcano."

It seems inevitable, then, that some future Pompeii is located in Puyallup or Enumclaw. Archaeologists may find perfectly-preserved flat screen TVs and hard drives with their data still intact. Maybe whole families, even whole neighborhoods, will be preserved for posterity as they were in Italy, with horrified looks on their fossilized faces, bodies frozen in postures of agonized deaths.

Of course, everything we do and everything we *don't* do is a gamble. We never know for sure if we will make it home tonight— or if home will still be there. We may *all* be wiped out someday, like the dinosaurs.

But I don't think about that as I paddle back to Tramp Harbor with that giant blue and white volcano smiling full in my face. I just think about the oneness and the everythingness and the momentary perfection of the planet as seen from a kayak in the East Passage.

I want to come back tomorrow and see it that way again.

Tango Charlie

High pressure has set in, as it almost always does this time of year, in late July. There is some haze, but the visibility is still well over 50 miles. It is easy to see details on Rainier, and what magnificent details they are. The huge active volcano is snow covered, even at the end of summer, down to 10,000 feet or so. Since it's over 14,400 tall, that means that almost a vertical mile of it is still bright white. Thirty-five or forty square miles of high snow are seen in contrast to blue sky and blue water. Magnificent.

From most of the beaches on south Vashon there is an awesome view of "The Mountain" as we locals call it. From the water it draws your eye like nothing else. On land you are always trying to find a place where you can see it better.

Port of Tacoma, a busy and growing destination for container ships and bulk carriers traveling to and from the Asian markets, lies directly northwest of Rainier's broad flanks. Seen from Tahlequah, the Mountain seems to grow out of the port. Looking at a satellite photo or map of the port, you can see that the prosaic view from Vashon is deceiving. There is a lot more there than you can see from six miles away. The enfilade arrangement is viewed end-on and so the islander or kayaker misses the full truth.

Ocean-going vessels enter the sound near Port Townsend and follow the Puget Sound Traffic Lane down the east side of Vashon, past the Point Robinson light and into the port. The narrowest part of the sound is at Point Robinson, but south of there it widens considerably. The channel itself is a wide highway, marked by buoys and electronic navaids, monitored by the Coast Guard, and can only be seen on charts. The boundaries are real, but they are invisible.

Ships mostly stay in the traffic lane. Kayaks are better off somewhere else.

Rule 9 of the United States Coast Guard Navigation Rules reads *"(b) A vessel of less than 20 meters in length or a sailing vessel shall not*

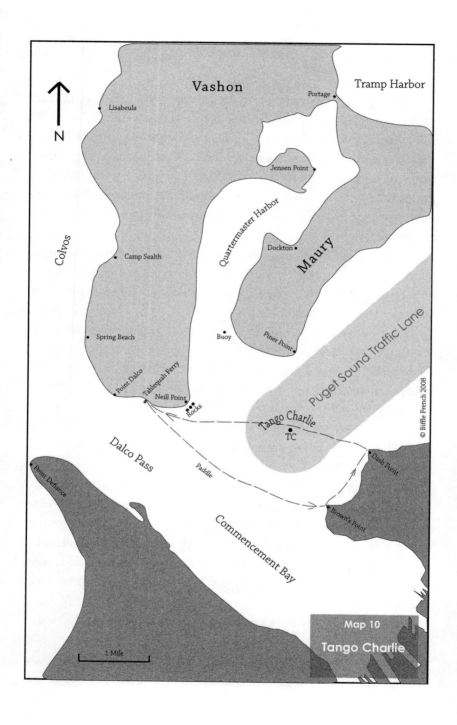

impede the passage of a vessel which can safely navigate only within a narrow channel or fairway." In other words "kayak beware" or "kayak skedaddle." If a kayaker is crushed like an empty beer can twixt hull and surface and then ground to hamburger by the propulsion system, leaving only tiny bloody bits of fiberglass and Polartec in the wake, well he has only himself to blame.

I start this day's paddle heading from Tahlequah to Piner Point, but along the way a more ambitious jaunt starts to fester. It's only 7:00, and I have nothing before my conference call at 11:00. I have never been to Brown's Point or Dash Point. And after all, it's just over there. The only thing between where I am and where I'd go is the invisible, abstract traffic lane.

It's four miles from my beach to Brown's Point, an eight-mile round trip. At my normal paddling speed of 4 miles per hour, that's about two hours of steady paddling for the round trip. Of course winds and currents can change that by a lot one way or the other. Especially the currents.

As I carefully pass across the traffic lane, looking both ways for something a million times my size and traveling at four times my top speed, I see a yellow buoy off my left side. It's some distance away, but I decide to visit it on the return, it being an interesting object in the middle of a great expanse of water, which is otherwise devoid of interesting objects that are not self propelled, and faster than kayaks.

I visit Brown's Point and Dash Point, and I judge both of them to be rather less interesting than I imagined seeing them across the water. Most things are. The Brown's Point light is stuck on the top of a cheerless, drab, squat cubic building. The park is small and appears to be used mainly as a doggie bathroom. There are some people fishing unsuccessfully off the beach. Confused about the location, I ask a boater if I'm at Dash Point. He doesn't know, but his girlfriend is hot, so I check her out.

"That's the Puyallup River over there," he offers. It's a couple of miles away. His boat can probably move 50 miles an hour, compared to my four or five, so the distance doesn't matter much to him. I am already tired – and late – enough.

"Thanks," I say, and smile. My dark sunglasses conceal the fact that I'm completely ignoring him and scoping out his date. He has no information I can use, but I always try to make the best of any situation.

A middle-aged woman carrying fishing gear volunteers that I am at Brown's Point and Dash Point is the one to the northeast. It's about a mile over there but the trip looks more interesting than the current location and I am already planning to be zombie when I get back, so I light out. Dash Point turns out to be more of the same. Once there, a Vashon-bound kayaker is at land's end. Time to head for the barn.

So I turn left. Remembering the buoy, I pick it out in the distance and aim for it. It is roughly on my way home anyway. It doesn't look that far away. Probably nothing to see, but why not.

After paddling toward it for a bit, I notice it is not getting bigger as fast as I expected. I quickly develop two hypotheses. Either it's farther away (and therefore bigger and more interesting) than I imagined. Or else it's not, and I am just going slow, which means I will soon be run over by a container ship. I check my wrist GPS and see that I am making much better than my normal 14 plus minute mile, so maybe this trip will be more interesting than I thought.

I have tried to plan for a 90-degree crossing of the traffic lane, since I don't want to spend any more life-threatening time today than necessary. In theory, the safest place is the center of the channel, since Rule 9 says that ships should stay as far to the right in their lane as possible.

The buoy marks the center of the lane. It looms quite large as I approach. It is bright yellow and as I get closer I try to guess how big it is. Objects at sea have no scale unless there is another object of known size next to it to measure against.

I can make out the identifier as I approach. Black letters proclaim it as "TC." "Tango Charlie" that is, in the NATO Phonetic Alphabet.

A strong current carries me towards it, and I see its wake in the flow downstream from me.

As I close on the buoy I see some odd shapes on the deck. Some kind of machinery, I guess vaguely. What kind of machinery could be on a buoy? But this is a big one, it must be at least ten feet tall, much bigger than the red one in Quartermaster. I guess a big buoy like this has some mysteries. I am about to solve them.

I vaguely realize that I am missing something. The scale is all wrong. Those are not parts of the buoy at all. They are alive! There are three sea lions, two females and a male. And the male is huge. My brain gropes to process the size in the absence of something to measure against. Now I see that Tango Charlie is at least *twenty* feet tall, maybe more, and the platform is maybe ten or twelve feet across. The bull sea lion hangs off both sides of it. I've seen big sea lions before, but...

How can there be a sea lion that big? At once I see that he and everything else is even bigger than I thought. At the same time I understand that I am not looking at a California sea lion, but rather a Steller sea lion, which is a much larger beast. Small males grow to 600 kg, but really big ones like this fellow can top 1,100 kg, or almost 2500 pounds. That's a monster. I am on track to meet him.

A prisoner of the current and having committed somewhat to my approach, I find I am getting nearer to the bull and his harem than I intended, nearer than either of us is comfortable with. Thinking I was close earlier, now I really *am* getting close—and it is happening uncontrollable fast.

Suddenly, he slips into the water, leaving the cows on the deck.

I don't have any idea what's going to happen next, but I keep hearing what sounds like my own voice saying "Mommy." In my frozen mind a clear vision forms of a ton of angry, athletic marine mammal leaping out of the cold choppy water, landing smack on the lime-green deck of my kayak, and blowing his hot, fishy breath into my face just before tearing it off with his long, razor-sharp incisors.

"Mommy."

I alter course as much as possible to avoid the coming confrontation, trying to put as much distance between him and me as I can. I don't know where he is, and the fear of the unknown is the worst fear.

A swift, dark shadow races under my boat and the shock wave sends a "thump" through it. I am thumped by a marine mammal. Then a U-turn and back to the buoy. This time he smacks the bottom of the boat with his muscular tail fin. "SMACK." The boat shudders like Jell-O in an earthquake

No, wait, the fear of the *known* is the worst fear.

I'm at my closest approach now, about to widen the distance for a change. As I pass abeam the buoy his huge head pops out of the water. Keeping himself between his harem and me, he lifts at least a third of his massive body out of the water and holds it there. How he does it I don't know, but from that position he is twice as high as my head, maybe four feet of rippling shaggy mane and shoulders bobbing in the chop. Our eyes meet. Mine are full of frightened tears.

I know the attack is coming. I steel for it, not expecting to survive. I will be dead in two or three minutes, and I try to accept that. At least now I know how it will happen, something I've wondered about, off and on, for years. Helpless in the water, my former kayak's hull a pointless pair of floating watertight compartments with jagged fiberglass edges where my body was ripped free, I will become a grisly meal for the denizens of Tango Charlie.

Searchers will find the boat's broken hull later, pointy ends toward heaven, floating like the pair of 38-DDD falsies she carelessly discarded just before a our impromptu twilight skinny dip at Lake Travis all those years ago. A knee-jab to the groin of my imagination, a hip-check to my heart. Pancakes. I will become breakfast.

All this very much reminds me of the time my brother talked me into "boot skiing" down a slide zone in the Sangre de Cristos. He thought it would be faster than just walking back down, as indeed it was. That event, even more than some others, really brought home to me the importance of having a good decision-making process.

A loose river of pebbles, sand and silt had formed in a high couloir from millions of years of erosion. The constant arrival of new material had piled the whole mass to its material dumping angle, the maximum angle it will stably pile to. (Every material has one. For instance asphalt can be piled to forty-five degrees, while garbage sloughs off at thirty. I do not know the dumping angles for live fish or dead kayakers.) Any object placed on top of a maximum-angle pile exceeds the material dumping angle and slides down to start a new layer at the bottom. That object was going to be us.

"Have you really tried this before?"

"Of course, many times."

"How do you do it?"

"You just walk out there, then when you start to slide you kinda hunker down a bit to keep your balance. That's all there is to it. We'll be at the bottom pretty quick. Just try to stay on your feet."

"Well, OK, but it looks dangerous to me."

"We'll be fine" he said, grabbing my arm and launching the both of us on a desperate ride that still causes me to wake up sweating 30 years later.

As the magnitude of our miscalculation and the depth of our commitment became obvious, I yelled "Have you really done this before?"

"Not really, but I've *thought* about it a lot. It *should* work!"

Funny guy.

Hoping for a merciful miracle, I paddle as hard as I can. The big fellow begins a loud sea lion bark. "Oy, Oy, Oy..." like Godzilla yodeling in Yiddish. Sea lion diplomacy. My last warning.

Straining and sweating I make hull speed, six miles per hour. The maximum effort makes me pant and I open my mouth wide to gulp the cool air. My heartbeat goes nonlinear. He watches me warily, barking his death threats. "And don't come back." We separate. I paddle, he barks.

We both know it is over now, and who the winner was. I keep some measure of pride by reminding myself that I maintained full bladder control during the entire encounter, something that was never assured. The current pushes me on. Home is less than an hour's paddle away and I've got to get my brain ready for that conference call.

Vashon Ferry to Dilworth

This final paddle completes my circumnavigation. The four miles or so from the Vashon Ferry dock to Dilworth point are the last little section in my orbit of Vashon. I have done it the hard way, really – a piece here and a piece there – except for the Colvos trip there never was a single one that even made ten miles. The reason is that I had to do it alone, and that usually meant out and back—back to the truck. Without help it's hard to spot the truck or the boat, and hitchhiking home is for younger folks than me.

So I made a patchwork circuit of the island, but there it is. And now it is finished. I know that a lot of people have circled Vashon, probably hundreds, and if it were a world record event it would not be an old man like me who has done it. I did it because I wanted to write this book, but more than that I wanted to do some paddling—Vashon is here and so am I, so here is where I have paddled.

Today is September 8th, less than two weeks from the equinox. The weather is still warm and beautiful, but the light is fading. Sunup this morning is after 6:30, so I do not get started as early as I might have. I get to the north end about 7:30, concerned that there might be traffic at the boat ramp. I needn't have worried, though, no one is there but me, and now I know why.

When the water level is above about eight feet, the bottom of the boat ramp is under water and launching a kayak would be very difficult, but launching a fishing boat off a trailer is easy. When the level is zero feet, as it is this morning, there is about a hundred feet of sandy beach between the bottom of the ramp and the water's edge. That's an easy portage for a kayak, but a major obstacle for a Boston Whaler, and a daunting haul even for an aluminum boat with detachable wheels. Most people aren't willing to work that hard. So I have the ramp to myself.

I pull the kayak off the top of the truck and gingerly carry it down the ramp. Whenever I see green algae on any surface it makes me con-

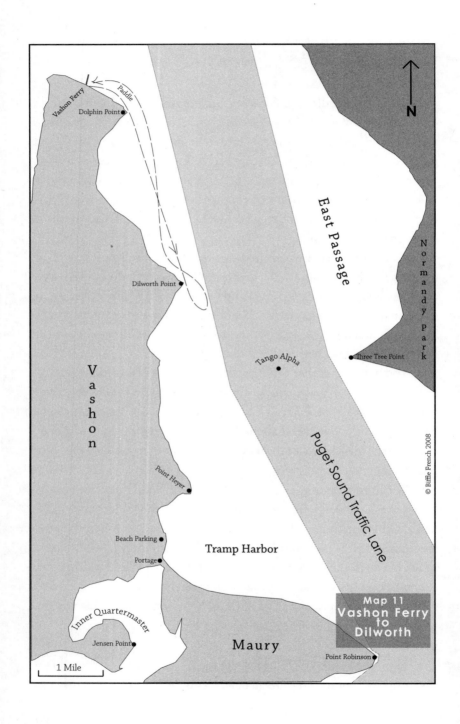

cerned, because algae is slippery stuff. I walk across the muddy, sandy, stream-covered beach and put the boat about ten feet back from the shore. Then I drive the truck back to the car park and lock it up.

There is already some wind-driven surf when I arrive, and it is too much to use the parallel launch, so I have to face the kayak into the waves and push off with my knuckles. That's easy when the bottom is sandy, as it is there, but the shock of the water on my hands is a surprise. "Damn, that's cold!" I say out loud, and my fingers sting for a bit.

When I am afloat I grab the paddle and feel that happy moment of control. I always warm up by rocking the hull several times in each direction as far as it will go. Then I lean it just past the tipping point and recover with a high brace to convince myself I can do it, should the need arise. *All systems go. Let's rock!*

The wind is from the north this morning and the current from the south, an ebb tide. That's the combination that gives the biggest waves, and sure enough they are out today. From the ferry dock it is a half mile trip to Dolphin Point, and I start for there.

Once away from shore I am in two-foot waves, which has not happened much this summer. I always like to paddle when the sea is as calm as a sheltered lake, but there is something exciting about kayaking in the waves. It is like skiing the moguls—more work, but you are moving in three dimensions instead of just two. This is a blue run, we are off the greens. I never paddle the black diamonds, but this is real kayaking. Summer is ending and soon there will be waves like this at least half the time.

As I turn southeast towards Dolphin Point I have the wind at my back. I estimate it at force 3 or 4, under fifteen miles per hour, but enough to add some interest to the day. I am surfing down the fronts of the waves a bit before they pass under me. Here at the north end of Vashon there is a clear path of open water all the way to the San Juans, fifty miles or more of fetch under the right conditions, so the little breeze stirs up much bigger waves than would be the case at the south end of Vashon under the same conditions.

"Fetch," in nautical terms means the distance that the wind blows over water. If breezes blow over a long stretch of water, then harmonics develop as the wave crests form. Where there are crests, the wind has a surface to push against, and that makes the waves bigger. As a wave moves a long distance it grows.

In the southern hemisphere there is no land at all between 56° south latitude and Antarctica. That leaves a zone whose narrowest defile is 360 miles wide where the winds are free to circumnavigate the planet, creating effectively infinite fetch. Fifty-foot waves are common, and rogue waves over a hundred feet high are a regular occurrence. Kayakers never paddle there.

At Dolphin Point I see flags arranged on a flagpole as they would be on the stays of a sailboat mast. At the top is the Stars and Stripes, then below that the Union Jack and Maple Leaf. Underneath those are two others that I don't recognize. All five are standing straight out.

Dilworth Point is straight ahead three miles away or so, and I decide that I will take the straight path. Paddling against the current is a chore, even with the wind, and I don't want to go any farther than I have to. It is getting to be a bit of a slog here, as I am only making twenty-minute miles —three miles per hour. Following close to the shore might let me see the local real estate better, but I am happier here in the open water by myself.

About half-way to Dilworth I see a day-glow orange zodiac with a shelter roof being piloted by two young men with beards. They look at me, I look at them, and now that we have seen each other I figure they will avert eyes and go away, which is the etiquette in Washington, but it does not happen that way. They aim their craft at me and push the throttle up, getting within hailing distance.

"Mornin'. We just wanted to know if you are doing any fishing today."

Now I understand who they are and the purpose of their friendly visit. I might be a paddling poacher.

"Gee, if I caught one it might pull me right over, don't you think?"

"Oh no, I see a guy fishing from a kayak out here every day. He just lets them pull him around until they get tired, then he hauls them in."

"Wow, I'll have to try that."

"I have a sit-on-top that I caught a *tuna* in once. You can do it. It's not really that hard. This other guy has a rod holder fixed to the top of his kayak. Makes it pretty easy to paddle or fish."

Tuna are some big critters. If I ever do decide to fish from the kayak, I really hope like hell the tuna stay away from me.

"I'll have to try that. Thanks for the info." Whenever the police approach you, always thank them for their interest. It makes them look at you in a different light. I smile and try to look as innocent as Mother Teresa. *Please go away, cops. I'm harmless, really.*

"Have a good paddle. Looks like fun."

"Oh, yeah, nothin' like it."

They wave and blast away in their iridescent Zodiac, leaving me bobbing in their wake, and as they disappear I see that their jackets have "WDFW" in stitched on the back in reflective letters. I watch to see who they will visit next as I struggle on toward Dilworth, but there is no other boat for at least a mile in any direction, so I quickly lose interest as they fade into the distance.

When I reach the Dilworth Point, the wind is so strong that it is hard to turn around. I stop paddling for a minute to take a drink of water, and am quickly blown around the graveled cape in the direction of Tramp Harbor. I've moved a couple hundred feet past it by the time I am able to change direction.

Now the wind is in my face. The brim on my Resistol-with-a-cork-cable-tied-to-it starts flopping around, and I wonder if today will be one of those times I am glad for the cork. A hat that floats might come in handy today.

I decide to follow the shore to ease the chore of paddling, since the wind is so strong. It now appears to be at the force 4 to 5 level, making paddling north even harder than paddling south was. I am moving with the current now, but it is nearly low tide, so there isn't all that much current to help me. The wind is whistling, though, and I am fighting to make progress. The GPS shows that I am making thirty-minute miles – two miles per hour, or half my no-resistance normal cruise speed. This is a real backbreaker, but I am still over three miles from the ferry dock, so there is no choice but to soldier on.

I try to stay near shore, but there are too many boulders. I see a lot of them, but there must be many more that I *don't* see. I give up on the idea of staying close in and strike out on the straight path again. There just is no easy way on a day like today. At least the open water path is shorter.

When I finally reach Dolphin Point I imagine that things are miraculously going to get better soon. But that is a faulty analysis. What happens is that now, instead of going directly into the wind, I am now dealing with a direct crosswind of almost twenty miles per hour. The waves that I was so easily cresting earlier are now breaking sideways over the deck of the boat. My summer spray skirt is useless against the onslaught, and water is coming in everywhere.

My shirt is quickly soaked, and my swim trunks soggy. I begin to wallow a moment of uncharacteristic self-pity as I think about how handy a rudder would be *just now*, even though I know I would not like to have to haul the stupid thing around the rest of the time. A rudder might keep me tracking better, and possibly save me from these crosswind-driven waves breaking across my deck, ignoring my spray skirt, and icing down my pants. Maybe a cabin cruiser is what I *really* need.

I have to stay away from shore until I am ready to land because there are hazards here as well, and I don't know this area well enough to avoid them. When I get abeam the boat ramp I quickly swing the bow around and run in with the surf. The soft sand stops me, but I am still in the path of the waves as they wash the beach. There's nothing for it but to get out of the boat and get the feet as wet as the pants are. I might as well be cold all over.

I carry the NC-17 over to the bottom of the boat ramp and unload it. I don't like to haul it up that slippery, rock-hard, barnacle-covered surface with a load. Anyway I've got to get the truck out of the car park and it's easier to carry all the gear up the steps with me now.

As I climb the hill to the parking lot I am a sight – purple swim trunks dripping seawater, long-sleeved T-shirt soaked to the chest, wet spray-skirt flopping around my knees, Resistol-with-a-cork-cable-tied-to-it soaked with sweat, fluttering in the breeze, and neoprene booties filled to the brim sloshing with every step.

A bearded man about forty years old is walking down the hill towards me. As we get closer, he develops an intense interest in the dead leaves lining the roadside. When we pass, he glances briefly, cautiously in my direction. A Texan would have looked me directly in the eye, grinned and said something helpful like, *"Whoa!—you look like pure-dee shit!"* This guy pretends that I am not even there, even though I know for sure he finds my appearance notable. One country, one language, different cultures. Morality is geography.

I'm exhausted now from the effort of over two hours of relentless heavy paddling, but somehow I manage to load the boat onto the truck and cinch the tie downs. I get in, soaking the seat. Then I grab a baggie full of Cheetos from my grub stash and jam in a mouthful, quickly turning lips, face and fingers an artificial yellow color. When I find my key I start the little engine, shift into first gear, turn left across the ferry traffic, and begin the climb up the big hill.

Suddenly I am just another guy with greasy, bright yellow fingers, driving home in wet purple swim trunks and wearing a funny hat. But what a day, eh? What a day!

How Long is a Coastline?

> *"...In the Empire in question, the Cartographer's Art reached such a degree of Perfection that the map of a single Province took up an entire City, and the map of the Empire covered an entire Province. After a while these Outsized Maps were no longer sufficient, and the Schools of Cartography created a Map of the Empire that was the size of the Empire, matching it point by point."* Jorge Luis Borges, On Scientific Rigor

A strong paddler with plenty of food and drink, one who chooses the right day and plans for the tides, might be able to circumnavigate Vashon in a single day. I imagine plenty of people have done it, although I am not one of them.

If I use dividers and measure around the circumference of Vashon Island as it shows on the NOAA Coast Survey Chart, I measure a distance of about 28 nautical miles, about 32 statute miles. The Colvos is roughly 12 nautical miles, or 14 statute miles. When I paddled the Colvos, though, my actual distance traveled was 18 GPS–measured statute miles.

Now if I calculate that ratio of map-measured to actual miles, I get about 1.3. So if that ratio holds, an average distance that a kayaker might travel to circumnavigate the island is about 41 statute miles. You can shorten that considerably if you take the straight-line course from Dolphin Point to Dilworth Point and from Dilworth Point to Robinson Point. It is just slightly shorter if you take the direct course from Dolphin Point to Robinson Point and bypass Dilworth Point completely, but that puts you into the Puget Sound Traffic Lane for much of the trip, which may be problematic.

Using the 18 mile estimate from Tahlequah to Vashon Ferry Dock and the GPS–measured values for the shortest other distances, I get something like this:

How Long is a Coastline?

Tahlequah to Vashon Ferry	18
Vashon Ferry to Dilworth	4
Dilworth to Robinson	6
Robinson to Tahlequah	8
Total	36

On the summer solstice civil twilight begins just after 4:30 a.m. and ends at almost 10:00 p.m. That's seventeen and a half hours of daylight, which should be plenty of time to paddle the 36 miles or so from Tahlequah ferry dock north with the current through the Colvos, around the Vashon ferry dock and back down the East Passage to Piner Point, only three miles from the finish line, assuming favorable tides.

At a steady four miles per hour you could theoretically do it in ten hours or so, and four miles per hour is no hill for a stepper. If you get back too early and still have some energy left, you can always add a bit of distance by just paddling the Quartermaster Harbor as well.

I've never tried it because, frankly, I think it's too hard for me. I'm too old. My kayak is too short. I have to wash my hair. My dog ate my homework. I had a flat tire. My Mom said "no." I'm not feeling well. It looks like rain.

But that does bring up the interesting question: exactly how long is the Vashon coastline? As unreasonable as it may seem to say this, that question can never be answered. Or rather, you could give the consultant's answer: "That depends."

There are several things that make measuring a coastline impossible. In the case of Vashon, of course, there are the tides. You can propose to measure the coastline at a particular tidal datum, say "mean low water." Proposing it and actually doing it are two different things, however. Standing on the summit of mountain A and measuring to the summit of mountain B can be done by several methods, and accurate technique will yield relatively repeatable results. But standing on a ten mile long beach and figuring out exactly where mean low water is at every point is a practical impossibility. In the end, though, that is a practical problem which means it is the province of the physical world and therefore *theoretically* might be solved over a finite area. The real difficulty is fractal.

A mathematician studying the issue may see the physical problem as unimportant, but he would still have to say that the coastline can never be accurately measured because of Heisenberg's Uncertainty Principle. It states that deterministic measurements of a physical system are not possible. That principle, which is one of the foundations of quantum physics, makes it clear that the more accurately you try to measure something, the less your improved accuracy converges.

Dip the thermometer into the coffee and the thermal mass of the thermometer changes the temperature of the coffee.

Use a satellite photograph to measure between Point Robinson and Piner Point with dividers set to 1 NM will give me a number, sure, but it will not be the coastline length, just an approximation. If I set the dividers to 0.1 NM, I will get a better number since I am following closer to the actual curves, but it will still be off. The smaller I set the dividers, the closer I will get, but the real number will still elude me, because there isn't one.

There is a very simple proof using the Koch triangle that shows the measured length across any natural surface increases continually with improved measurements, meaning that it is unbounded—that is to say, infinite. This contradicts another result from physics that claims that there is a shortest distance that can be measured. So it's a conundrum.

For the paddler who stays in close to shore and who finishes the trek by traveling in a straight line from Piner Point across the mouth of Quartermaster, the distance is roughly 41 miles. If you straighten out the curves, it will be shorter. The best strategy is to paddle the Colvos on the ebb and the East Passage on the flood. But if you get to Tahlequah with the tide above 8 feet, you will not be able to land there. Getting it right depends on timing the tides, as well as favorable winds. Whether you can do it all depends on you, of course.

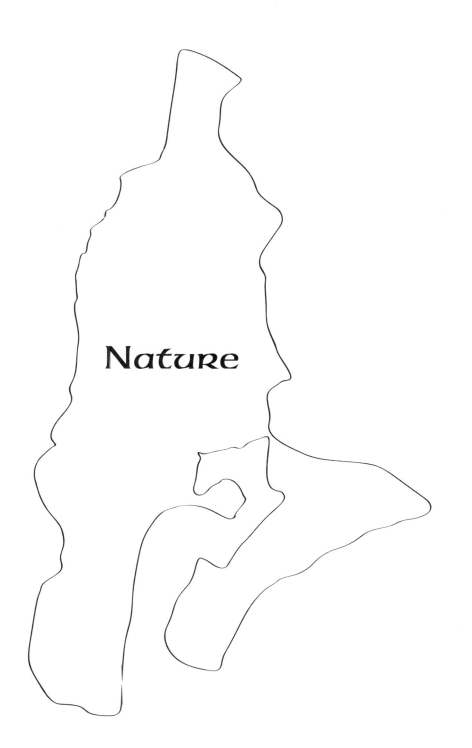

All science has one aim, namely to find a theory of Nature

Emerson

Earth

It is August now, as I write this, the best time for paddling and today is particularly beautiful. We pay for this sweetness with the dreary winter, but that is a cheap price.

I almost never kayak in December or January. I don't mind the cold, and it rarely gets cold here anyway. The real problem is the tides and then, of course, there is the wind.

Winter days almost never have a good tide during daylight. I need a tide of less than 8 feet to get on the beach, reasonably light winds and daylight.

From the first of December until the end of January there are less than ten hours of daylight per day. Of course, even if everything else were equal that would reduce the chances of low tide and daylight occurring at the same time. But if you look at the tide chart you will see that it's much worse than that.

In December there are only a couple of low tides below seven feet that occur during daylight hours. There are none below 6 ½ feet. If I get on the beach at 6 ½ feet with the tide coming in I don't have much time to paddle, and even if I launch as the tide drops below 8 feet on the ebb and then recover when the tide is approaching 8 feet again on the flood I still have very little time. That is probably moot anyway, because it will likely be too windy that day to do anything, and that 6½ foot low tide only happens once in daylight in December. During the depth of winter the lowest low tides all occur in darkness.

Of course, you can paddle in the darkness if you like, but I never do. The idea of hauling my boat over to Jensen Point for an hour's paddle in the windy, rainy darkness does not appeal to me. Paddling in open water at night, say in the East Passage, is somewhat dangerous unless you have a good light, since there is commercial traffic, big boats, that will not see you otherwise.

December is also the month when terrible wind storms are likely, especially around the solstice. High winds raise giant breaking waves at sea and topple trees on land. Gusts may exceed sixty or even seventy miles per hour. There is no place for a paddler in those conditions, no matter how brave.

January is just about the same, although by the last week of January we are already five weeks past the solstice and so there is more daylight. The last day of January has 40 minutes more daylight than the first day. There were four times in January this year where there were tides in the below 5' range that occurred in daylight, so things are starting to improve. But the weather is usually poor then, so I almost never go.

Ducks that came in the fall stay through winter, and they are wonderful to watch in their numbers. Surf Scoter, Goldeneye, Bufflehead and many others flock and fly low across the sound, using ground effect to improve their flying efficiency. If an airplane or a bird flies less than half a wingspan above a solid surface like water, then the drag force of flight is reduced significantly and it takes a lot less oomph to get the same speed. When I flew sailplanes in Texas, I got too low to get back once and I took a chance that ground effect would give me the extra distance to make it over the fence. That was risky, since if I didn't get all the way over I might have been decapitated. On the other hand it would have been no fun dragging that three hundred pound glider a mile back to the field across a lumpy cow pasture on a hundred degree day.

So ground effect is why you see the echelon fleets of ducks, geese, and cormorants low on the water, traveling long distances at high speed. They are taking advantage of reduced drag and flying easy. If you see them from a kayak, they are lower even than your eye level. You look slightly down on them from a distance and see the whole flock, speeding along like black fighter planes on a stealth mission.

February is a month that can go anywhere. I have seen my yard full with tulips one year and covered with snow patches for two whole weeks the next. By the end of February the day length is about 11 hours, that's still short but we all know that the winter blues are coming to an end. We can feel it.

Mathematicians like to label things. If "L" is the day length in hours, then ΔL is the rate of change of L. It's called the "first derivative" of L. The second derivative of day length, the rate at which ΔL is changing, written "$\Delta(\Delta L)$", is positive as well. That means that the rate at which the days are getting longer is also increasing—the days are getting longer faster.

At the beginning of January, the day length increases by about one minute per day. By the end of February that is up to about three minutes. The second derivative goes to zero on the spring equinox and then becomes negative after that. Day length increases by about four minutes per day during the third week of March. Then the days keep getting longer until the summer solstice, but at a slower rate. The day length increases by about three minutes per day for April, one minute per day by the end of May. The days just around the Summer solstice are only different from each other by a few seconds. Then the whole sequence plays in reverse, with the day length decreasing at its fastest rate around the fall equinox and barely changing at all near the winter solstice.

In February of this year there were fifteen days with tides low enough to paddle in daylight. If the weather is right, February can be a go about half the time. I wear a "ThermalStretch" wetsuit when it is cold and rainy. That's a brand name, and there are other similar ones, but the fabric is Polartec and Spandex. Rain rolls off and it's very breathable and warm. I have a Gore-Tex hat that I wear in winter to keep my head dry. I wear the Atlas Thermal Fit gloves from True Value, and they work better than anything I've tried. Even soaking wet, which they definitely will be, they keep your fingers good and warm in any temperature above about 40° F.

The duck and cormorant population seems happy to stay on at Vashon through February. Later they will become restless, but in February they are content to remain. Eagles, who are here all year in some numbers, start to arrive in strength now and build their nests. I have heard that they attack blue herons and take their rookeries but I do not

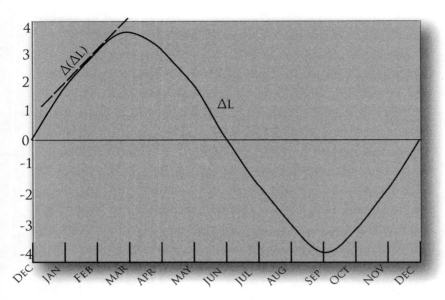

ΔL = Rate of Change
in minutes of daylight per day

(How many more minutes of daylight today than yesterday?)

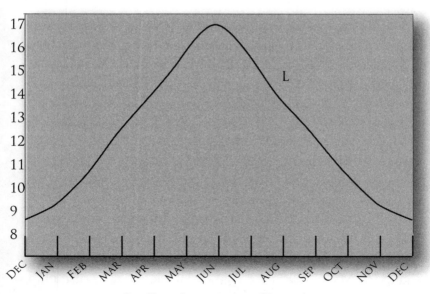

L = Day Length in Hours
(Sunrise to Sunset)

know if that is true.

When I lived in Vancouver, I heard loons all the time around English Bay, but I never saw one here until I started kayaking. Now I see loons in Quartermaster in February regularly, making their strange little cry.

In March the hummingbirds come back, and about ten years ago I watched a cloud of migrating hummingbirds come through my yard one March day. There were hummingbirds as thick as bumblebees around the lavender. They did not stay together for long, but went their separate ways soon afterwards. If you know their little calls, you hear them everywhere all summer, even if you can't see them.

From October until the 4th of July there is a phenomenon that occurs regularly on Vashon—the locals call it "rain." If you are from Texas, that is the same as what we call "drizzle." True rain, the kind that causes a driver to lose visual contact with the hood ornament, never occurs here.

Here on Vashon, if it is not windy, you can use an umbrella to keep dry, although most people have special clothing with "North Face" or "Columbia" stitched onto the front. It is convenient that here the rain occurs when it is cool enough to wear a jacket.

I remember often being faced with rain, real manly rain, in Texas. A flat parking lot is ankle deep after the first five minutes. The temperature is 90°, so a jacket is out of the question. There is a stiff 30 mph wind, making an umbrella, which no Texan owns anyway, pointless. Inside Wal-Mart or Target, people are wet, soaked to the skin like kittens who fell in the pool. The lucky dry ones stand in the door, waiting for a break, hoping the cloud doesn't turn green and then black. Such a thing, not even worthy of discussion in Texas, has never happened here in my 20 years of residence in the Northwest, but I'm sure that if it did, it would cause comment.

In March and in April, May and June the gentle Vashon rain need not deter a paddler. I do not like the wind, though, even when it is not Texas wind.

Nature

By May there are good low tides every day at some time, and it stays that way until November with very few exceptions. Days are very long now, although it can still be windy. Most of the ducks are gone and the cormorants are leaving as well, headed up north where it's cooler. They have no need for the sweet summer weather. Our ospreys have come back and started their nest. I see them, the consummate fishermen, always headed home with a fresh catch. They never seem to miss.

Migrating geese are back now, honking everywhere obnoxiously. Their eggs will hatch soon and they will be teaching the young to swim and fly. I have seen an eagle that was flying casually overhead swoop down vertically with no warning in an attempt to make away with a gosling who was at the fresh water in the scupper delta. The adults ringed round and warded off the attack, but it was quite close and very surprising and exciting for me to watch. I had seen eagles fish for years, but I had never seen one take a creature on the land. My neighbor, Frank, told me he saw an eagle take a friend's cat off a roof, so it is probably more common than I know. Another neighbor reports watching a pair of eagles hunt grebes, with one flying above to frighten them under, and another swooping in for the kill from low on the water when they surface. These giant raptors are predators of opportunity, they take anything they can get.

In June, the days are the longest and the best paddling times have started. It still rains frequently in June, averaging just slightly less than in May, although there are often several days of good weather in a row, and heavy rain is rare. Every day in June has long periods when a paddler can get on the beach below eight feet. Most days have daytime tides that are quite low, often below zero feet and the spring tides can go to almost minus four feet. Sandy beaches are everywhere. Counting the half hour of twilight there are almost 17 hours of daylight, paddlers almost never have to stop.

In the summer the water can turn "hazy," with visibility close to zero some days. Other days the water is crystal clear and the shallow-water paddler can see the bottom with no restrictions. Often the haziness is due to algae blooms, although there are some times when it looks more like silt kicked up by boaters or wind-driven waves.

July is much like late June, except that the 4th brings out every boat in the Puget Sound. They zoom around everywhere, towing children on rubber floats, fishing, crabbing, racing and cruising. Boats of every size and description are in the water, from fast Zodiacs and Cigarettes to hundred-foot steel motor yachts, and the wake surf is constant. Since the wakes come from every direction, the effect is one of constant, incoherent waves—big and small, all chopped up like on a gusty day.

I don't really like to paddle on the 4th, since there seems to be no safe place in the water for a kayaker. I've tried to stay close to shore, only to have speed cruisers race through the boulder fields between me and Neil Point, just missing the Point Rock by luck, and never even knowing it was there. Boaters on that day seem to be overcome with irrational exuberance and their teeming masses are best avoided. If the 4th comes on a Friday or Monday, the madness lasts until the final afternoon of the three-day weekend, when there is a race for the boat ramps and the marinas.

July is when the salmon come in their numbers to the Puget Sound. Two years ago I was returning from Point Dalco along the beaches at Tahlequah in about six feet of water, when I saw a large number of big fish swimming just to my left, a couple of feet below the surface. They were going much faster than I could, whizzing by in their hundreds.

I thought that the school would end, but it did not. For as long as I paddled, the migratory millions came. The shape was like a big pipe, and about four or five feet in diameter. Not a fish swam by himself, but every one kept in the bounds of the highway, churning on with a purpose – continuation of the species. Nature's imperative must be obeyed.

On Monday, August 19th, 1805 Meriwether Lewis, who was staying with the Shoshones, wrote about the salmon in his diary

"From the middle of May until the first of September these people

reside on the waters of the Columbia where they consider themselves in perfect security from their enemies as they have not yet ever found their way to this retreat; during this season the salmon furnish the principal part of their subsistence and as the fish either perishes or returns about the 1st of September they are compelled at this season in surch of subsistence to resort to the Missouri, in the vallies of which, there is more game even within the mountains."

The Shoshone lived far upriver in the mountains, but ate salmon every day for months, and the Indians of the Pacific Northwest depended on them even more. I do not know how many salmon there are now compared to 1805, but I suspect that it is many fewer. That is what happens, though. We can never go back to the world of 1805, where the wretched Shoshone hid most of the year in mountain valleys, subsisting on berries and nuts while living in desperate fear of their slave-hunting Blackfoot neighbors, nor should we wish to. If Cameahwait, who wanted rifles more than anything, could walk our path instead of his, I know which one he would choose.

July is normally the driest month, with less than an inch of rainfall expected, and its mean temperature is 65°, compared with 66° for August, which is hottest and also quite dry. The most reliable paddling weather of the year is in August, but the light starts to fade then.

July is the time when the jellyfish start to appear, small at first and then more and larger. There are a lot of types of jellyfish, and even my friend David, the marine biologist, can't recognize them all by sight. Most of the photographs that someone might use to identify a specific jelly are taken from the side, but the paddler has a view of any jellyfish that is quite different from the one seen by divers and underwater photographers. Only one can sting you: the Lion's Mane jellyfish.

As I paddle every day during the summer months, and I am always attracted to the jellyfish. But I am *amazed* by the Lion's Mane. This enormous scyphozoan has been known to grow its bell to seven and a half feet in diameter and its tentacles to 120 feet. These are the largest jellyfish known and only rarely occur below 42° N latitude.

The Lion's Mane is one of nature's deadly beauties. Many divers have been stung—death is rare but the stings are painful. In general, though, whatever the Lion's Mane stings, it eats. A large, fleshy mass the color of an egg yolk before it starts to cook is contained in a clear sac of bodily fluid. All around are tentacles, extending far below, where the paddler can not see them.

The Lion's Mane is rather rare, and sighting a big one is a notable event. Other jellies are more common and sometimes seem to be everywhere. The Moon Jelly, another scyphozoan about ten to fifteen inches across, is beautiful to see, with its four windows in the middle of the bell. In August their populations increase dramatically and in clear water you can not paddle anywhere without seeing them. They suffer from surf and fast ebbing tides, sometimes dieing by the hundreds on our beach.

Plenty of other, smaller jellyfish grow in the waters around Vashon and a paddler who likes to watch them will always have a treat in the summer.

At the start of August we have fifteen hours of daylight, but by the end there are only about thirteen and a half. There are good low tides every day in August, but the lowest are not nearly so low as in June. The spring tides in August normally don't drop to minus two feet, so they are far above the minus four feet seen in June. Still, that's plenty low, and gives lots of opportunities for the paddler.

By August the bird migrations are in full swing. I see cormorant and duck populations beginning to build, and I also see terns in the air and on the water, as well as many birds I don't recognize. I often wish I could take a birder with me when I paddle, since it is hard to get close enough sometimes to recognize water birds with the naked eye, and I can't bother with binoculars when I am paddling.

One of my favorite birds is the delightful art-deco Caspian Tern with its raucous war cry. When they sail through Dalco Pass, they seem like a hungry invading army, each soldier ready for action. I hear that raspy shriek in the evening and it fills me with a primal excitement, as if

I were a sky hunter, feasting on the squirming bodies of my prey.

The fall equinox, on the 21st of September takes us back to twelve-hour days. Day length change is at its maximum here and people who live far above the Mason-Dixon line know that the long darkness is coming quickly. Still, September itself is one of the best months of the year, like a demand for surrender delivered by a beautiful maiden, willing, delicate and smiling.

In September the tidal clock shifts back toward the winter schedule again, and there are more days without good low tides during day-

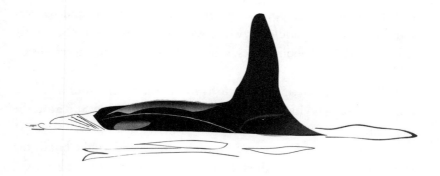

light hours. At the end of September, though, something else is about to happen. Something wonderful.

Fall is when the pods of Orcas come swimming through Puget Sound, usually in October and November. I've never been close to one in a kayak, but I have been as close as you can legally get in a Boston Whaler.

We saw the fins like black sailboards coming our way from the direction of Tango Charlie. My neighbor had been fishing, and his Whaler was in the water. I walked down to the beach and he motored up. "Want'a to go look?" he asked, unnecessarily.

"Damn right I do." I said, sensing a once in a lifetime opportunity. I climbed aboard, getting shoes and pant legs wet in the process. We sped out on an intersecting course, like a formation rejoin, but with the other fellow not caring a bit whether you got there or not.

Don's Whaler has a 75 hp engine, which is plenty powerful. Watching him from the window, I always wonder how much it costs him to keep that big fellow running. I think we were making maybe forty miles per hour or more as we scooted across toward Owen Beach, hoping to get as near as possible before they were gone for good.

Killer Whales travel at an amazing speed and with the ease of a porpoise. They don't seem to be working, but shoot along like torpedoes. Sometimes they dive after a meal, and sometimes they just scoot along at the surface, dorsal fin in the air like a giant flag.

I had not expected to be going for a boat ride just then, the whole idea being rather impromptu, and I was not dressed for it. By the time we got close to the Orcas my ears were hurting from the icy wind and my wet feet were numb. I would not have turned back for anything, though, so I just stuffed my fingers in my ears, ignored my feet and smiled whenever Don said anything to me.

We got to the intersect just in time. Another thirty seconds and they would have been hopelessly out of reach. The Whaler could barely match their velocity and I watched with the wonder and amazement of a child as the pod outpaced us. Their black and white kitten faces bobbed up and down as they sped effortlessly by, hunting and traveling, looking for kill, greedy for sport. Then they were gone, around Point Defiance and into the south Sound. We could not catch them, only watch and grin as they disappeared.

They come every fall, although it is not always in the daylight and their traveling speed is so great that you have to be looking just when they arrive or you will miss them. Sometimes we neighbors phone each other. "Whales! Just coming by the grain elevators!" Sometimes none of us see them, only to read about it in the paper later, when they are already gone.

The good paddling is all done by November and everything is different then. The mean temperature in November is 45°, compared to 53° for October, much colder. November averages almost six inches of rain, more than any other month and double October's three. There are only a few days in November with good tides, and by the middle of the month paddling starts to give way to thoughts of other things.

I lived at the equator for a couple of years, where the seasons are two: rainy and not-so-rainy. It is hot in the day and not as hot at night. There is no drama in such a place, although we *did* have monkeys and really big snakes. To be on Vashon, where the changes and rhythm are as intense as they are, is a joy and a privilege. Tomorrow is different than today. Next year it will repeat again, but not exactly. The planet is like a giant Mandelbrot set: it seems random, but there is a pattern that guides and provokes the randomness. It cannot exceed its range, but our puny lives are too short and our vision too weak to see what the range really is, so it is always surprising us.

AIR

I am in the Colvos Passage, just north of Point Dalco, and I am blind. All around me I can hear boats, small fishing boats, big cruisers, enormous tugs with their barges, but I can not see them. Nor can they see me, because the visibility has dropped to zero. Not one of us, in fact, can see another unless we come very close – something we all hope doesn't happen.

I knew it might turn out this way when I started my paddle, but I didn't assign it a high enough probability. "Chance of fog" or "Areas of fog" are words they might have used on today's weather report. I lack the strength to watch television, though, since it always makes me retch. So I miss the weather, and I also miss the stories of murder, rape, victimization, political malfeasance, and the constant drumbeat of adverts for wonderful items that you would not be able to live without, if only you knew they existed.

To paraphrase Marx, and I think that in today's world the reformulation is particularly apt: "Television is the opiate of the masses."

I could check the internet, and sometimes I do, but the Weather Channel often tries to show little dancing figures, like electronic cockroaches, or embedded television sets that try to take over my computer, and that always leads to bouts of cursing. So I could have done, but I did not.

Rather, I struck out, awed by the gentle glassy sea and overcome by the visual excitement and mystery of the lowering ceiling. Little fronds of diaphanous cloud curling across the far shore beckoned me, the utter calm of a fog-prone morning tested my resistance and overcame it. Now I am blind, lost and out of ideas.

A Chinese friend had trouble with navigation in the days before Garmin began to offer cheap car GPSs. "Why don't you get a compass for your car?," I suggested, thinking that might help. "That will not work," she said, "even I have ten compass I still lost." I remember that conversation as I sit here, being drawn up the Colvos at a rate I can not

BEAUFORT SCALE OF WIND SPEED

Force	Wind (Kts)	Classification	On Water / On Land
0	<1	Calm	Sea surface smooth and mirror-like
			Smoke rises vertically
1	1-3	Light Air	Scaly ripples, no foam crests
			Wind vanes still, smoke drift indicates wind direction
2	4-6	Light Breeze	Small wavelets, glassy crests, no breaking
			Leaves rustle, wind vanes move, face feels wind
3	7-10	Gentle Breeze	Large wavelets, crests begin to break, scattered whitecaps
			Leaves and twigs move, light flags extended
4	11-16	Moderate Breeze	Small waves, 1-4 feet, numerous whitecaps
			Small tree branches move. Dust, leaves & paper lifted
5	17-21	Fresh Breeze	Moderate waves 4-8 feet, many whitecaps, some spray
			Small trees in leaf begin to sway
6	22-27	Strong Breeze	Larger waves 8-13 feet, whitecaps common, more spray
			Larger tree branches move, wires whistle
7	28-33	Near Gale	Sea heaps up, waves 13-20 feet, foam streaks off breakers
			Whole trees move, resistance felt walking against wind
8	34-40	Gale	Long 20 foot waves, foam blown in streaks
			Slight structural damage occurs
9	41-47	Strong Gale	High waves, sea rolls, dense streaks of foam, low visibility
			Trees broken or uprooted, considerable structural damage
10	48-55	Storm	Waves 30 feet with overhanging crests, sea white
			Trees broken or uprooted, considerable structural damage
11	56-63	Violent Storm	45 foot waves, foam patches cover sea, low visibility
			Trees broken or uprooted, considerable structural damage
12	64+	Hurricane	Waves over 45 feet, driving spray, low visibility
			Trees broken or uprooted, considerable structural damage

estimate, surrounded by all manner of invisible dangers and wishing to hell that I had just one.

As it turns out, the fog is patchy and either the low cloud moves away somehow or I move out of it, drawn along on the current. In a few moments I see Vashon's west shore and paddle for Spring Beach.

Fog is a rather predictable phenomenon, and is most likely when the temperature is below the dew point and winds are calm. However, like any act of nature, what some model says does not necessarily have any relation to what actually happens in the event. No model of any natural phenomenon can ever be accurate or deterministic, because every computer program is necessarily simplistic, static and finite, whereas the natural phenomenon it pretends to predict is richly complex, highly nuanced, self-affecting, dynamic, probabilistic and infinite. That is why weathermen always talk in probabilities—it is because they know that they can never know. They *can* predict that they can not predict, so they do that, instead.

This day, it is the calm that surprises me. Other days it is the wind.

The Beaufort scale is a measurement of wind speed that is based on observable phenomena. If you see smoke rising vertically, you know that the wind is calm. If you see large trees being uprooted and flung into the next county, you know that it is breezy.

Beaufort divided his scale into what he call "forces." He gave each force a descriptive name and identifiable phenomena to help observers estimate wind speed. A force 5 wind of 17-21 knots, he named a "fresh breeze." He also provided a description: "Small trees sway, moderate waves, many white foam crests." I don't like to paddle in a force 5 wind, and I *really* don't like to paddle in winds any stronger than that, although small craft advisories are not usually issued until force 6 is reached, at 22 mph.

I find it hard to make forward progress directly into the wind anytime there are whitecaps, although waves are generally not a hindrance. You can paddle in waves, but if the wind is pushing on you harder than you can push on the water, you will not be going anywhere.

If the wind is going your way, and you are surfing down the fronts of the waves, you have the power of nature at your command, and you feel that the paddling is easy and fast. That is all fine if you don't plan to reverse direction later. But if you do, watch out, since you may not be able to.

The actual force of wind, in the sense of physical force, not Beaufort force, varies as the square of the wind speed. Compare, for instance, a 10 mph wind with a 20 mph wind, twice as fast. Now 10 squared is 100, but 20 squared is 400. So a 20 mph wind is four times as forceful as the 10 mph wind. A 40 mph wind is *sixteen* times as forceful as the 10 mph wind. For myself, I like to paddle when the winds are less than 10 mph, since I know that I will be able to get back home, barring some other disaster.

You can calculate the force of the wind on a kayaker and you can calculate the force of the kayaker's paddles on the water. That is generally limited not by the kayaker's strength, but rather by the viscosity of the liquid and the size of the paddle surface. For me, though, it is enough to know that if I am paddling forward at maximum overdrive and still proceeding aft, then I am in some really deep shit.

I have had that happen sometimes, usually during powerful gusts, never during sustained winds so far, but it still got my attention. March, April and May when I am really itching to paddle, and when it seems just a bit "extra breezy," are a dangerous time for me. I have more than once convinced myself that "It's OK. The wind is not that strong," even though I could *see* the whitecaps in the sound. If, after launching, the kayak can not be controlled and you are floating sideways through a boulder field, what do you do? For myself, I cuss. It really seems to help.

FIRE

Of course there is no place at all in a kayaking book for a chapter about fire—I know that, OK? On the other hand, it doesn't make sense to break "Nature" up into just "Earth, Air and Water." That feels kind of incomplete doesn't it? Anyway, I wrote this piece, and there's nothing you can do about it. I tried to keep it pretty short. You don't have to read it if you don't want to.

Ω

Here on south Vashon, people fish for firewood.

Immense log barges, made of hundreds of freshly-cut, trimmed tree trunks lashed together and pulled by straining tugs chained to the lashing, ply the Dalco Pass regularly. The lashings are not perfect, and even if they were it would be impossible that a log would not escape now and then, which they do.

Stormy weather or fine, the tugs lose a log here and there, and they float in the Dalco Pass, abandoned property, salvageable by the first claimant. I have one neighbor who uses a wooden dinghy to row out and pick up his prize. He drives a sixteen penny nail into the soft fir and bends it over a bowline loop tied in a stout line that he then attaches to the stern of the dinghy. When all is fast, he rows home, log in tow. It is sweaty work, but it is free firewood.

The tug captain may see logs escape, but there is no action he can take either to prevent the loss or recapture his charge. His chains are hundreds of feet long and must be kept quite taut. The log barges are assembled in a contained area, but now he is in open water. The captain has his hands full just making the tow—trying to corral one stray out of the thousand logs in his care is just not a paying proposition. He lets them go. There is no other way.

When firewood fishermen get back to the beach, they have to leave their logs in the water. A wet fir trunk weighs several hundred pounds and can not be lifted without heavy equipment, which we have none of. So the firewood fisherman lashes the beast to his bulkhead and waits for the water to rise. At high water, he pulls it in close, where it stays until the tide goes out again. When the tide is low and the log is close, he saws it into rounds, splits it in place and tosses the green splits up onto dry land. This year they must dry, next year they will burn.

So it is firewood from the sea that keeps the beach people warm in winter, a tradition that goes back very far into the past. It is the oldest ones who expect it and appreciate it the most. One of my neighbors is nearly 80 years old, but I hear his saw going all summer as he gets in his crop of fire.

All winter, fires are burning in the wood stoves of south Vashon. Fire from the water.

WATER

Adolescent preoccupation with sex and low job satisfaction among teachers have led many otherwise intelligent people to believe that the moon circles the earth and the earth circles the sun. Neither is exactly true. If you understand it that way, it is not your fault – you were never given all the facts. Here they are:

The earth and moon are tethered by the Giant Bungee Cord of Gravity.

Pretend you are God, grab one or the other, swing the pair once around your head and then off into space. See how the one does not circle the other, but instead they both circle the center of their mass. Since the earth is much more massive, the center of mass is inside the earth, but not at the center, it's about 3/4 of the way out from it.

Now suppose the big one (the Earth) was a water balloon. These are enormous, massive objects, whirling around their center of mass, tethered together by gravity. Nothing slows them down, and once God has let fly, nothing speeds them up (nothing much, anyway, this is only physics, after all – not Math). How would the water balloon one look? Would it be round?

No. It would be shaped kind of like a very nicely-proportioned pear. It would be thinnest near where the bungee is attached, and it would be fattest opposite that, since the centripetal force of the spin would cause all the water to collect away from the center. If you want clear evidence of this, fill a balloon with water, tie a string to it, and sling it around you while walking in a tight circle for a bit. Check the shape. When you get dizzy, sit down.

So this is the first part of how the tides work. The Earth and moon sling each other around their collective center of mass. The water wants to go to the outside of the circle. Since the Earth is also rotating at about 15° per hour and there are continents obstructing the flow, all the water can never get where it's going before it's time to go somewhere else, otherwise the tides would be a lot higher.

The place on the earth opposite the moon is where the biggest amount of water piles up. We call that the *high* high tide.

In addition to the centripetal force of the system, there is the gravitational force of the moon which acts on all the particles of the earth, but not with the same force. It acts on the close ones much more than on the distant ones. So the place on the earth just between the center of the earth and the center of the moon bulges out toward the moon. That's hard to detect when it's rock, because the bulge is small, but when it's water, the bulge is easy to spot. We call that the *low* high tide.

Since the earth rotates on its axis, the points of the bulges move with respect to points on the earth. So there are two high and two low tides per day, a higher high on the side opposite the moon and a lower high on the moon side. To find the location of those tides, just draw a straight line through the centers of the earth and moon. Where that line intersects the surface of the earth there is a high tide. The *magnitude* of that tide is controlled by the relationship between the sun, earth and moon.

The Earth/moon system has the same relationship to the sun that they individually have with each other. The whole Earth/Moon/sun system is rotating around their collective center of mass. The sun being a whole lot more massive than the puny Earth/Moon, though, that particular center of mass is inside the sun itself (although not at the center).

The gravity of the sun also has a tidal effect, but it is less than half that of the moon. When the earth, sun and moon are aligned in syzygy, at the full and new moons, the effects of the moon and sun are added. This is the spring tide. When they are at 90°, at the half moons, the effects somewhat cancel each other and tides are smallest. This is the neap tide. So the magnitude of the tide changes every day, from neap to spring and back again.

The highest high tides also cause the lowest low tides, because the water has to go somewhere. If more water goes to the high tides, there is less water where the high tide isn't, so you get the lowest low tides.

The tidal gradient is the rate of change of the tide, in units per hour at a particular time of day, say 6:14 PM. The tidal gradient changes constantly from zero to maximum flow and back to zero. Its value depends on the difference between the high and low tides. If the high tide is 11.46 feet, and the low tide is -1.36 feet as it is today, a change of 12.82 feet, which for this cycle occurs in roughly 6 hours, then the *average* gradient is about 2 feet per hour.

But that's deceiving since the gradient is zero at dead high or low tide and builds to a max in the center, calming to zero again at the end. The tide does not rise or fall at a constant rate. Near peak high or low tides, there is very little movement of water. Slack water, with no current at all, occurs after the moment of dead high or low due to inertia in the system. Somewhere about the middle of ebb or flood, there is a build to a maximum flow, which diminishes after it is reached. The maximum gradient for today is probably more like 3 feet per hour, which is a gigantic amount of water flowing in or out of the narrow Puget Sound and right by Vashon Island.

There are lots of places where the tide is more dramatic than Vashon, of course. The Bay of Fundy in Nova Scotia has tide swings of 53 feet. Hangzhou, China, where my wife was born and raised, has a tidal river, the Qiantang, fed by an estuary on the flood. The estuary acts as a big funnel, and on spring tides when the gradient is steep it acts like a nozzle causing a thirty-foot high wall of water to move up the river at fifteen miles per hour. Because the area is a popular tourist destination, especially for many Chinese, and the temporarily-dry river bed such an interesting place, people who don't know to remain in the tide watching area are killed every year by the great tidal bore.

Some places have almost no tide swing at all. Galveston, Texas, in the Gulf of Mexico has only about a three-foot tide. Due to differences in bathymetry some locations on the earth actually have no measurable tides at all.

According to the NOAA charts, the tides at my house vary from plus fourteen to minus three. That is only the calculated values, though and changes in barometric pressure or high winds can make for even more extreme tides.

Of course, we probably never see a real seventeen foot tide in one swing, but fourteen feet is not uncommon. That happens in about a six hour period. To put it in perspective, if perspective is possible for such an Olympian event, consider that the Puget Sound is about 90 miles long from Olympia to Everett. It is not very wide, maybe five miles at the widest point, but think about the whole thing getting fourteen feet deeper in such a short time. Most of that water will flow between Seattle and Bainbridge, and everything south of the Narrows will flow past Vashon, which sits in the middle of the Sound like a stopper in a bathtub.

The tidal flows around Vashon can be quite strong as planetary volumes of water move through the narrow stretches of the Sound. Currents under the Tacoma Narrows bridge are listed on the charts as five knots or so, but I have GPS-measured almost seven on many occasions. That's because the chart value is an average, based on the how much water is flowing, while the real value is more probabilistic based on bathymetric facts (i.e. the shape of the bottom at a particular location) that interact and cause additive effects in certain areas.

$$\Omega$$

The maximum speed of a boat with a non-planing hull, like a kayak is called its "hull speed." It is easy to calculate a rough estimate of it.

If H = the hull speed in knots and

lwl = the waterline length in feet,

then the theoretical hull speed for a boat is usually given by the formula:

$$H = 1.3 \sqrt{lwl}$$

So for instance my boat is 17 feet at the water, and the square root of 17 is roughly 4.1. Multiply that times 1.3 and you get about 5.3. So my hull speed is about 5.3 knots, or 6.1 miles per hour.

This hull speed rule of thumb is based on the wave propagation speed for a wave with the length of the hull waterline. That's a severe limitation, by the way, since it takes a lot more length to get just a little more speed. For instance, if my kayak was twice as long as it is, 34 feet, let's say, then the hull speed calculation still yields only 7.6 knots. That's why fast boats have to have planing hulls. Once the boat rides on top of the bow wave, the hull speed limitation disappears.

As I mentioned above, the hull speed of my boat is about 5.3 knots or about 6 miles per hour (one knot = 1.15 miles per hour). Hull speed means it won't go any faster than that in the water. If you could pull it behind a go-fast boat like a giant water ski, it would go faster, of course, once it got up on top and planed. But that would take lots of power, since it's not designed for planing. Anyway, if you are paddling a non-planing boat, hull speed is as fast as you are going to go, although the true maximum speed might be slightly more or less than the rule of thumb calculation given above, since good or bad design can also play a part. In general, though, long boats have higher hull speeds than shorter boats, and the speed increase is roughly proportional to the square root of the length.

My GPS-measured top speed in slack water with no wind is a little over a ten minute mile, which is a little under 6 miles per hour, about what you'd expect from the hull speed calculation. That is a sprint, and I can not keep it up for more than four or five minutes without going into oxygen debt and having my old heart beat harder than is probably good for it.

A ten minute mile is an easy jog on solid ground. I used to be able to run a seven minute mile no problem, although that is unlikely these days. Marathon runners put in times of just over six minute miles for the whole 24-mile slog, and milers run under four minutes regularly. You just can't do that in a kayak. It is a good workout, but more stately.

Nature

People on the shore watching your progress think you are not in a hurry no matter how hard you are paddling.

If you follow my argument so far you realize that the current in this part of the Puget Sound can at times be much faster than you can paddle. Very good if you and the current want to go the same way. Very bad if you don't. A kayak under those circumstances is only a leaf in the rapids. Poseidon is in the driver's seat. The paddler is only a passenger.

Probably the most dangerous area for any boater near Vashon Island is directly under the Tacoma Narrows Bridge. It is there that the current is fastest, and it is there that there is a lot of large immobile stuff to run in to. Sometimes there is a standing three-foot-high wave in places, an indication of a powerful tide rip. Big, powerful fishing boats, expensive sailboats and work boats driven by professional crews have all met disaster under the Narrows Bridge. There are better places to kayak.

I love to catch the rocket current coming *out* of the Narrows, since that allows you to get into the main flow up the Colvos. That outbound, or northern current happens when the tide is falling (ebb tide). But when the tide is flooding, the flow is the other direction, to the south, and if you get south of Gig Harbor, say, you could have a tough time getting back north of there. You could get even sucked into the Narrows if you let the situation deteriorate too far.

If you kayak in a place every day, you get to know the currents and you have an idea what to expect. If it is your first time, then may be in for something you didn't bargain for. Maybe something real interesting.

The currents around Vashon behave in surprising ways. In general, but not necessarily at a particular time or a particular place, there is a current that flows clockwise around the island. The reason for that is the shape of the Y, which causes most of the water flowing out of Narrows to shoot up the Colvos instead of turning right at Dalco Pass.

As the incoming flood tide rushes past north Vashon and down the East Passage it finds an easier route than down the narrow Colvos.

The flow passes Maury Island and some flows right, up into Quartermaster Harbor, to keep the level there. But once it reaches Point Dalco it makes another decision. Most of the water flows through the Narrows toward Olympia, but the rest turns right again and flows north, up the narrower Colvos Passage.

As the outgoing ebb tide flows north out of the Narrows, some of it turns right and heads over toward Des Moines. But most of it flows straight north, up the Colvos. When it gets to land's end at north Vashon it is pulled inexorably on by the fall in the water level.

In addition to the more or less coherent big currents, there are smaller eddies that can help you or frustrate you. Often there are back eddies near the shore that move in the opposite direction from the main line of current. That may result from the V-shaped bottom which allows the water flowing in the center of the channel to move with no restrictions, while the shallower water near the shore is hindered by the steep, boulder-strewn floor.

Rounding Point Dalco from the east when a strong tide is ebbing is impossible since there is a powerful and turbulent flow of as much as five knots from the northwest. When the tide is flooding, that current is still there, but it is much slower, which allows you to pass through. Out in the middle of the Y the current moves strongly north during the ebb, so a kayaker can hitch a ride at Point Defiance, turn right at Spring Beach, and follow the back eddy back to Tahlequah.

Micro currents like this one, and larger stable flows exist throughout the Puget Sound. In general if the current is going your way the best place to be is in the middle of the channel where the flow is coherent. If the current is going against you, the best place to be is right at the shoreline to benefit either from back eddies or at least get help from the frictional effect of shallow water and nearby land which cuts the current speed dramatically. Sometimes, though, no matter what you do, you can not go where you want to go until the tide reverses.

If you are close to the shore you need to watch out for submerged boulders which are everywhere. In a current with no wind or wakes you can spot standing waves that clearly mark the downstream side of a boulder. When the water is choppy, that trick doesn't work. Because of the reflective water surface, you typically can't see a boulder until your face is directly above it. By then, if it's a hazard you would have felt the impact.

$$\Omega$$

In Homer's Odyssey, the Hero Odysseus, describes the giant whirlpool, Charybdis, which he and his crew had to sail by in a narrow straight. On the other side of the straight was the giant monster, Scylla. They feared Charybdis more than Scylla, and favored Scylla's side to avoid being sucked to the bottom of the sea. As they passed the demon, she plucked some of the crew off the boat and ate them as they screamed, begging Odysseus to save them. Still, the rest did get by, although now they were somewhat short handed.

Irresistible currents of planetary strength striking continuously against underwater cliffs hundreds of feet high cause turbulent flows of staggering ferocity all around Vashon Island and throughout the Puget Sound. Water may flow directly upwards as it strikes steep walls. Whirlpools and huge rapid-like flows challenge the boater, and especially the kayaker whenever the tide gradient is steep. These are tide rips.

Vashon/Maury Island is two mountains rising out of a deep underwater canyon connected by the small paved Isthmus of Maury. The deepest part of inner Quartermaster Harbor is only six feet at mean lower low water. The deepest part of the East Passage about four miles east across Maury, the depth reaches 130 fathoms, (780 feet). The flat-bottomed channel of the Colvos is 65 fathoms (390 feet) deep in many places, and its sides are sheer, underwater cliffs, popular with freezing scuba divers.

An 800-foot-deep river flowing at five miles per hour confronts a shallow. Or comes to a steep wall. Or is forced through a narrow opening and empties onto a wide underwater plain. Irresistible force meets immovable object.

If you've ever stood near a fast river in the mountains after a flash flood, you've heard the grinding sound of giant boulders being whisked along like billiard balls by the stream. The flow in the East Passage rivals the Amazon in volume, and unlike the Amazon, which is mainly constrained by its own soft mud delta and has therefore some control over its route, the tidal flow of three feet per hour filling or emptying through the rocky chasm of the East Passage and piling up into the Colvos is not at liberty to change much at all. It goes where it has to go.

A pebble in a stream leaves a wake.

In the middle of the Y, just at the point where the stream divides between the Colvos to the north and the Narrows to the south there is a steep, rocky underwater mountain almost 300 feet higher than the nearby bottom. Its summit is still more than 100 feet deep at mean lower low water, but it is a formidable obstacle to the tidal flow rushing in through Dalco Pass or out from the Narrows. This nameless submerged eminence is 500 feet above the bottom of Dalco Pass—higher than downtown Vashon is from the water's surface. It is about four times as large as the Burton Peninsula, and forms an immense immersed cascade almost twice the height of Niagara Falls that twice daily disgorges the contents of the south Sound into the Colvos across its steep rocks. I like to call it "Mount Dalco."

Tidal currents flowing across Mount Dalco are forced upward. Because the same volume of water must pass through a much smaller volume of space in the same time, the flow speed must increase. It is just like putting your thumb over the end of the garden hose. You do not stop the water—you just speed it up, so it flies. Mount Dalco speeds and redirects the colossal flow.

Paddling through Dalco Pass, especially out in the middle, when the tidal gradient is really steep is one of the more interesting experiences you can have while kayaking Vashon. It can also be one of the

NATURE

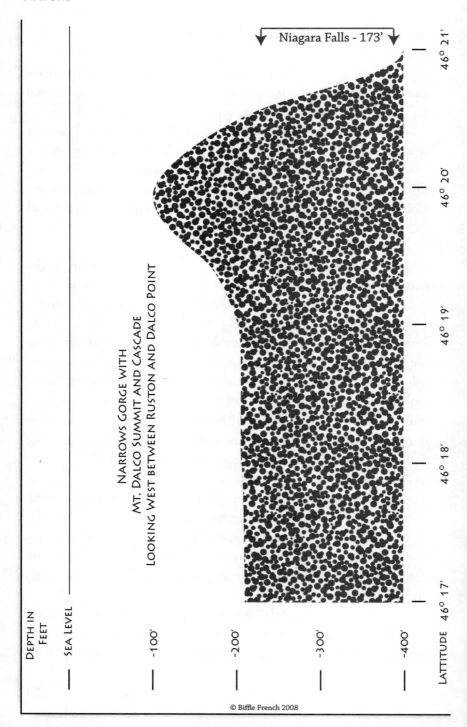

scarier ones. The Mount Dalco Rip is not a place for the new kayaker. If you don't have a lot of time in the boat, stay in calmer waters.

I have been on scene a few times when the Mount Dalco Rip started to awaken. Until I understood it, I was amazed to see an actual *dome* forming where water was being forced directly upward as it flowed across the peak, like holding a garden hose just under the surface of a swimming pool. A vertical flow of increasing ferocity forms when fast tidal currents impinge on the mountain.

In a few minutes the dome loses coherence and breaks into a standing wave. Whirlpools begin to form everywhere. Fast eddies and back eddies confront the paddler. Progress ahead may preclude an easy return. Once I paddled myself weak trying to pass the Mount Dalco Rip at Point Dalco and get into the northbound current flowing up the Colvos. In the end I had to give up. Now I know the way, but that day I could not find a route in.

Tide rips are everywhere in the Puget Sound. The same bathymetric phenomena cause all of them. Conceptually, the idea is simple – water striking a submerged object forms a wave. But exactly how that is going to play out in a particular place, at a particular tide level and gradient, in a particular wind situation is hard to predict unless you paddle there all the time.

...*With a weeks Provisions we began the Examination of the Inlet. We found it trend nearly South for about 4 leagues and in that Distance preserving the Breadth of One Mile, we were there induced to stop to Breakfast in hopes of enticing two Indians who had deserted their Canoe and fled into the Woods to come to us—she was hauled up close to the Trees and before we went away some Beads Medals and Trinkets were put among their other Articles as a proof that our Intentions were friendly.*

Lt. Peter Puget,
LOG ENTRY DISCUSSING THE EXPLORATION OF COLVOS PASSAGE FROM THE OPEN LAUNCH, MAY 1792.

Clearcut

When Mr. Puget sailed down the Colvos passage in 1792 in his well-armed launch, the land on both sides was covered with old growth forest. It was part of what used to be called the "Great North Woods," a giant conifer forest that covered the coastal areas of northern California, Oregon, Washington, British Columbia and southern Alaska and extended inland as far as far as there was good rainfall.

There were Indian villages on Vashon, as everywhere in the region and the locals burned driftwood for fuel, caught salmon and clams and netted birds. In Texas that year the hegemonic Nahuatl-speaking Comanches kept the tiny Spanish-speaking population bottled up behind the adobe walls of Bexar. They held the Athabascan-speaking Apaches as tributaries until many years after the Anglos arrived. But the Salish-speaking tribes of the Puget Sound area were a little gentler. These were civilized fishing people who lived in villages, spoke dialects of the same root language and shared a common culture.

Jefferson expected that it would take a century after Lewis and Clark for Americans to filter into the West. Instead, it happened almost overnight. As soon as news of the successful expedition spread throughout the United States, land fever gripped the nation as never before. Visions of free acres put Americans on the move.

Texas, which both Jefferson and Jackson thought was included in the Louisiana Purchase, had 200,000 Anglos by 1830, dwarfing the tiny Mexican population of only 2,000 souls huddled in San Antonio to protect each other from scalp-hunting Comanches. California, Oregon and Washington began to fill up quickly. Americans were on the move. By 1850 there were 100,000 Americans in California, ten years later the population quadrupled to almost 400,000.

San Francisco and other towns needed timber for building, and local sources were quickly exhausted. But Washington had plenty and it was easy to ship it by sea down the coast. Easy and lucrative.

So the clear cut of Vashon began. From about 1850 until just after the turn of the century, Vashon trees, along with timber from the rest of Washington went to California. The Golden State's citizens were flush with yellow metal and they spent a lot of it buying up Washington forests to build their new cities.

By the beginning of World War I, Vashon was mostly clear cut, with almost every mature tree removed, and no old growth trees remain on the island today. Photographs taken of the island in the 1920s show farmland where large stands of trees now stand. It is a testament to the immense regenerative power of nature that about 75% of Vashon is forest right now, up from zero less than a century ago. Barring a major forest fire or extensive new development, that percentage may never substantially decrease.

Farming began on Vashon in the late 19th century and at one point strawberries were the principal crop. A glut of strawberries caused prices to drop and many of the farmers eventually abandoned their fields. I have heard stories of a strawberry blight as well, but I haven't seen a source for it, so that may not be true.

Apples were another cash crop that was tried with some success, and the Wax Orchard operated a successful business until fairly recently. The Wax family sold their somewhat-neglected orchard to Misty Isle farms in 2005 and it was plowed up, burned and replanted with grazing for cattle.

Hippies discovered Vashon in the 1970s and brought forth the next major agricultural effort, marijuana husbandry, the most successful money crop since the last of the old growth trees. That business has slowed some in recent years as the population has increased and fields are harder to hide. In 1997 a Vashon man was arrested for having an underground marijuana cultivation system, housed in a buried container with automatic watering and powerful grow lights. As often happens in these cases, he couldn't keep his mouth shut and a "friend" ratted him out to the heat. The police clearcut his forest.

BLACKBERRIES

Luther Burbank, the mad genius of horticulture, was 36 years old when he got one of the stupidest ideas any plant breeder ever had. "I'll introduce a noxious weed that will take over any sunny location in the western United States with giant, thorny, unkillable vines. Maybe people can make some pies.," he wrote in his diary, "They'll thank me."

And so the Himalayan Blackberry, as he called it because he did not know it was really from Germany, was intentionally introduced to our innocent homeland. Like the rabbits introduced into Australia, like the starlings and sparrows introduced into the eastern U.S., another wacko environmental dilettante struck a blow at the fabric of nature. And it still resounds.

He could just as well have introduced cobras.

Wherever there is sun, the devil weed grows. And where it takes over, sun is assured, since it never allows any competition. Unchecked, and it is hard to check it, the vines become thickets fifteen or twenty feet high. A mature plant can have a root eight inches in diameter with suckers radiating out from it. Vine tips root, forming new plants yards from the parent.

The delicious berries attract birds, deer, mice, rats and kayakers. A purple dye is left on their fingers, lips and tongue to mark their sin. The seeds remain viable after a trek through a digestive system and sprout in any sunny location where they may happen to land. The flowers are self-pollinating so once the plant is established, it can develop offspring on its own.

"Crazy Luther" put in his first blackberry patch in Oregon around 1885, not wanting it to spread to Santa Rosa during his lifetime. He died of a heart attack in 1926, when the plants were just outside of town. Today they cover most of the ground from Cabo San Lucas to Anchorage.

Vashon suffers dreadfully from the evil vines. "They always come back," says one frightened and depressed gardener, a faraway look in her eye. "They always come back."

Vashon

Big Butts

Normal people, people like you and me, don't live on islands. Strangers come in the summer and get taken in by the romance of it all: the water, the Mountain, the quaint little town, and yes, the ferries. Visitors see the ferry as a boat ride, something that's fun. Islanders see the ferry as a bulwark against the outside, something that keeps *them* out. Except that it doesn't of course. *They* can buy a ticket just like *we* can. *They* can buy a *house* if they want to.

Instead, our moat just keeps *us* in. Want to go to Wal-Mart? Get in line. Kid got a soccer game? Get in line. Got to catch an airplane? Get in line. Sometimes it reminds me of being in the military and having to wait in a long queue to get an injection. That big guy up there, the one who can crush you like a bug, he gets *his* shot and passes out cold. It gives you something to look forward to as you wait your turn.

Every few years some group of developers eyes the open land on the Kitsap peninsula and trots out the idea of a bridge across Vashon. The last time was ten years ago or so, and the proposal was for a floating bridge that would have turned Cove Road into an eight-lane freeway. It would have terminated at Three Tree Point, in Normandy Park.

Now Vashon has never had a bridge and as an educated guesser, I am guessing that it never will. A bridge to Vashon is an engineering fantasy. If Vashon were in Dubai, where money is like water and citizens interests count for nothing, somebody *might* figure out how to build such a bridge. But not here.

For starters, you would need two bridges. One would go across the Colvos and the other would cross the East Passage. Stipulating that the Colvos bridge could be done since I don't want to waste time on that argument, let's consider the East Passage bridge.

In the East Passage, the proposed route terminates in an expensive neighborhood whose homes grow in value daily. Normandy Park wants a bridge like Maury Island wants a gravel mine.

At Fauntleroy the lack of a second ferry slip creates constant schedule slips and occasional disasters, but the political will against a second slip (as well as lack of interest on the part of the state) has prevented one being built for fifty years now. If we can't build a second ferry slip, how can we ever come together enough to build a bridge?

But even if the politics could be resolved, there is still the pesky question of engineering feasibility. The East Passage is almost 800 feet deep in places. If the pilings were placed just at the outer edges of the Puget Sound Traffic Lane, then the Vashon side piers would be in 600 feet of water, which would make any bridge pilings the deepest in the world. The deepest bridge pier in the world today is the 242 foot deep pier on the Bay Bridge in San Francisco. That pier, though, is buried in mud for most of its height. It does not stand that high in fast-moving water.

East Passage bridge pilings would be about the height of the Space Needle (605') considering just the *under water portion,* taller than almost any structure in the State of Washington. Powerful currents would try to topple them, and unless the underwater bases were the size of football fields that would surely happen. I don't know how deeply they would have to be buried in the mud.

But that's just the underwater part. A lot has to stick up on top, as well, to hold the massive cables for the 8000' span that would be required to clear the Puget Sound Traffic Lane, which passes under any possible bridge route. The bridge would have to be high enough to accommodate ocean-going vessels, including the largest container ships headed for the busy Port of Tacoma—typically about 200' above high water. The traffic lane obviously prevents a floating bridge, (the original proposal) so that won't happen, either.

So the bridge supports would have to hold up a six-lane or eight-lane roadbed 200 feet or so high, and 2000' longer than the longest suspension bridge in the world, the Akashi-Kaikyo bridge in Japan, which is 6000'. From top to bottom the piers would be at least 1200 feet high or so, taller than all but six of the world's tallest buildings, and none of those carry a heavy load.

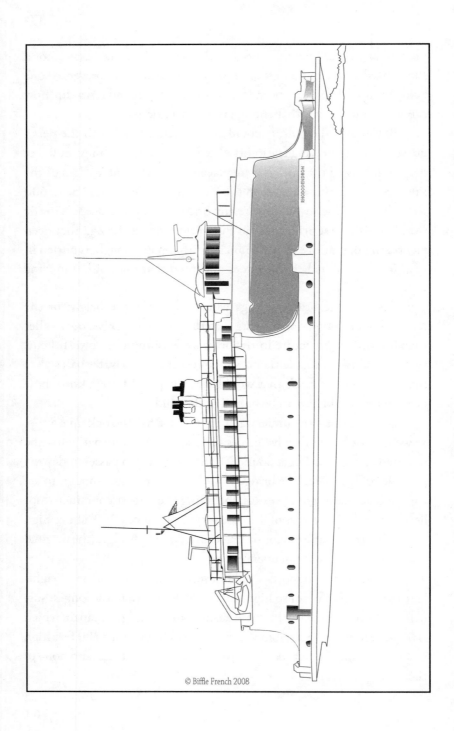

And this bridge, far past the limit of today's engineering science, would be constructed across a widening active fault in one of the world's major earthquake zones. Not to mention that this would happen in a state that can't keep open all the roads it already has.

Even if such a bridge were really feasible, and I believe that it is not, the cost would be many billions of dollars, and the per vehicle toll would have to be *at least* $30 in today's money. The result would be the most advanced bridge in the world, all so a few developers can open a little more land on Kitsap and Vashon Islands. This is masturbation.

So there never will be a bridge, and the ferries are the only game in town. Well, not exactly. There *is* a small airport, plenty of private boats, and some guys even have helicopters. But even for them, weather prevents a lot of trips, and they usually ride the big boats with the rest of us.

There was boat traffic to Vashon long before Mr. Puget sailed down the Colvos in his launch. Salish-speaking Indians of every tribe made dugouts and paddled them everywhere in the Sound.

Once the white population of Vashon was established, various small operators began to offer ferry service and the small independent services gradually grew into what used to be called the "Mosquito Fleet." Those independently-operated boats were all passenger-only craft, but as Vashon's population increased and automobiles became more common, people wanted to be able to bring them onto the island.

Captain Alexander Peabody formed a company called the "Black Ball Fleet" that offered regular car ferry service starting sometime in the 1930s. Black Ball operated as a private business until after World War II, when Captain Peabody wanted to raise fares during a time of high inflation. He was losing money.

The citizens of Vashon, having been trained during the Roosevelt years that somebody else should pay for everything, balked at the increased fares and withheld their business. At the same time, Peabody's boat crews struck due to Black Ball's inability to increase their wages, and ferry service ground to a complete halt. Olympia began to stir.

Vashon's citizenry, not being able to make the connection between their unwillingness to pay a fair price for something and the sudden unavailability of that thing which could no longer be sold to them at a loss, got the attention of state politicians, probably the last time that ever happened. Of course, they didn't really care about Vashon, which even now only a few of them can find on a wall map. But Black Ball served the entire Puget Sound and the whole edifice had begun to crumble.

So a deal was struck. Washington State bought Black Ball and Washington's last experiment in private enterprise before Microsoft was killed like a fat slug on a prize rose.

Today the ferry system is an institution and for better or worse it rules our lives. Five years ago ferry service to south Vashon was severely reduced as a cruel method of punishing *someone* for voting in favor of ending the license tab tax. Disregarding Vashon's suffering, our state legislator spent more time this year trying to get a law passed allowing "Dogs in Bars" than getting that hateful measure ended. They really don't care.

I used to ride the Kalama and Skagit, two passenger-only boats, downtown every day. These are crowded buses of the sea, with two decks full of passengers.

One day a deckhand confided to me that these were "not the most seaworthy craft in the fleet" and after that I began to sit much closer to the door, or stand there if I could not find a seat.

You never know what to expect with the ferry service. One morning we passengers were filing into the Kalama as usual, when the unexpected announcement was made that the boat was "full." And no one else could load.

"OK, that's it, we're not taking any more passengers. New rules."

We were pondering this when two more passengers, a tall attractive woman who is some kind of an attorney and her associate, a young man, arrived at the base of the ramp.

"Sorry, we're full. You guys take the next boat."

Ignoring his command, they pushed past and entered the unaccustomed spaciousness of the Kalama.

"What do you mean 'full'? There's room for fifty more people in here."

"Yeah, but there's new rules. We can only allow 150 passengers now. That's from the top. You guys have to get off."

"We will *not!*" she said, drawing herself up and assuming an imperious tone. "If you want us off, you'll have to get the sheriff to come and arrest us."

"Jeez, I don't want to do that. Plus it will make everybody late. Please get off. Just come earlier tomorrow."

But the impasse remained. The sheriff was called, and a deputy arrived straightaway.

"What's going on?"

"We won't leave unless you arrest us. You have to take us in," she said.

"Jeez, I don't want to do that, miss. Can't we talk about it outside?"

"No way, not unless you arrest us."

The deputy signed a sigh of deep resignation. "OK, I'm placing you under arrest. Now let's all get *off* the *boat.*"

The three walked down the ramp, the tall lawyer lady smiled the blessed smile of the righteous martyr, the sad deputy brought up the rear. The deck hand raised the ramp, but we were still close enough to hear.

"I changed my mind." said the deputy. "I'm just going to give you a citation."

"*WHAT???*" She was livid. "We expected *hand*cuffs! We expected the *squad* car! You *lied* to us!" Now I understand that lawyers don't think like I do, but those are not complaints I would ever have made.

The next day we found out that we were national news. She had gone to the media and *they* in turn had called Washington State Ferries for an explanation of what *really* happened. Before it was all over, it made the New York Times.

But the spinmeisters at WSF got there before us. Their take ran something like this:

> "Spokesmen for the Washington Ferry Service say that they regret the incident, but that changes have become necessary. Originally 18 inches per passenger were allotted on the bench seats in the passenger ferries. However, current passenger size trends require that they increase that. As a result, they were forced to reduce the number of passengers per boat."

As we read this, we were stunned. "Are they saying that they did this because our...our...butts are too big?" the lady next to me asked?

"I think that's what they're saying, yes. I think the implied headline is 'Big Butted Ferry Passengers Might Sink Boat.' They really had no choice. They did it for our own good."

Fiestas

In his fascinating book, "The Labyrinth of Solitude," Octavio Paz talks about life in Mexico in the 1960s, where many villages had none of the basic services or infrastructure that we had here in the United States. He describes discussing finances with the mayor of a small town.

Paz asks the Alcalde now much money the town has to spend in a year and gets the answer that it is about 3000 pesos, since even though they are poor, they do get some help from the Federal Government and the Governor.

When Paz asks how the money is spent, the Alcalde tells him that it is mostly on fiestas. That is unavoidable, he says, since they have two patron saints.

Of course, there *is* no government of Vashon. We are a tributary province of King County. On being given the Three Choices we chose the Tribute. The County only takes, they do not give. There is no fiesta money, not a penny. We are lucky to still have our lives.

But we do still have fiestas – no one can stop us.

Unlike in Mexico where it is fiesta season all year long, we limit our party time to the sweet warmth of the summer, when the days are long and rain is unlikely. That is to say "when rain is *less* likely," which is different.

The rainy season ends exactly on the 4th of July, and that coincides with the Boat Fiesta. We call it the Hydroplane Race. Of course, it's not really a race and there are few, if any hydroplanes in it. It's more like a bunch of sadists with really loud boats zooming counterclockwise around Vashon starting at 4:30 a.m.

The whole point of the thing is to let the people who stayed up until 2:00 a.m. the night before celebrating the arrival of independence day know that now it's really *here!* Time to get up and pop some *firecrackers*.

Of course I don't really do the pyrotechnics thing anymore, but old people can't sleep anyway, so I get up when the first unmuffled fiend powers by. I am waiting for it with eyes already open. I know what's coming. That front Cigarette shooting by, flames belching from straight pipes, is like the early robin of spring. There are a lot more behind him.

I hear him ripping down the Colvos, against the current, a distant buzz, like thunder in the next county. It is there now, but soon, very soon, it will be here. Piano, crescendo, forte. One Sooner ahead of the herd, but a stampede comes on behind.

So I get up, I stand at the window and I watch the parade. Because that's what it really is – not a race but a parade. "I have a *boat*. I took off the *muffler*. Now I am a *macho* man."

As a kayaker who once flew supersonic jets, I try to imagine what it must be like to drive the front Cigarette boat. By 4:00 he is at the ramp and full of nervous energy, ready to float his craft. It's still dark, but twilight is only 30 minutes away. The truck has backup lights— they will do. His friend backs the trailer and they crank out the cable —it is ready.

Key in the ignition, boost pump on, starter engaged, the baritone roar sounds. Even at idle, the compression wave pounds his chest, not just a sound, but an epiphany—time to rock and roll.

Most multi-engine airplanes have throttles with wooden balls as hand grips at the top of the control bars. Pushing the ganged throttles all the way forward toward the firewall, hitting the stops, is called "balls to the wall." Takeoff power. Full burner.

The boat driver points his bow seaward, then he carefully moves the twin throttles forward. The torque and RPM have to build at a constant rate to avoid a stall. Now the powerful engines are gulping all the air and fuel they want. The roar builds, he feels the acceleration of 1000 horsepower forcing his head back into the rest. Balls to the wall.

Later, as he passes Tahlequah, I am in the window watching, but he does not know it. People used to ask me, after I landed "What's it like, doing acrobatics in a little airplane like that?" What could I say, really? Go there, do that, then you will know.

I almost never paddle on the 4th of July anymore. That has become a hassle. The 4th is a better day to watch and listen, not to paddle. You can paddle then if you want, but a person could almost walk across boats in any direction and the water is so choppy with wake surf that it's just not quality paddling.

Vashon used to be covered with strawberry farms which is purportedly the origin of the Strawberry Festival. I think it is because we have no patron saints, but everyone can believe what they like.

Octavio Paz talks about how Mexico is lost because there is no Philosophy. In a way, I think *we* are lost, or at least we suffer, because we have no saints. We have no saints and we have forgotten our heroes. Now I am not a religious person, and never have been. But now that I am older I do wish Vashon had a patron saint. At least we could all agree on *that*. As it stands, we can't agree on much of anything.

Strawberry Festival happens the weekend after the 4th of July. That is a bunching together of fiestas, where they might arguably assuage more angst if they were a little farther apart, but there it is. The ferries fill up, Vashon Highway is closed to traffic and turned into a pedestrian mall, and for two days kitsch and small town fancies dominate everything.

There are parades, and what wonderful parades they are. There is a tractor parade. A couple of antiques and lots of riding lawn mowers. There is a kid parade. Are you a kid? You qualify. There is the military hardware parade. Always a big hit. But there *is* one act that is a Vashon original. The Thriftway Drill Team.

Yes, shopping carts. They go straight. They go in circles. They twirl, they dance, they do wheelies. Funky, cute and original. Some say it is a little shopworn these days, and in fact I haven't been to the Strawberry Festival for a while, but the last time I saw it, I was impressed. It is definitely Greatest Home Videos material.

Strawberry Festival is the last official fiesta of the year, but there is one more.

Motorcycle Day, the VITT or Vashon Island Tourist Trophy, has no known sponsor and the date is an official secret since everyone except a few enthusiasts hopes the bikers will stay home. The Chamber of Commerce claims it is apocryphal.

But for a biker event, it is really quite sedate – Vashon is not and never will be Sturgis. You don't just ride a bike into town and you don't just ride one out, either. You have to get on a ferry and there are only so many ferries per day. Like it or not, traffic to Vashon, in and out, is controlled.

Most of the bikes that come to Vashon that day are vintage. Some of them are real knockouts. I have a neighbor who rebuilds motorcycles, and he has a 1968 AJS that looks like it just came off the factory floor, except that the paint is better.

The bikers line Vashon highway with their rides, and then they walk up and down the line oohing and aahing all the *other* bikes. Then they go to the bar, which has a long line out front.

After Motorcycle Day, which happens near the end of August, the fiesta season, such as it is, is over. Labor Day comes and goes, but the good weather sticks around a few weeks longer. Then the rains come and the days are short again. Boaters put up their boats and most kayakers put up their kayaks.

I paddle till Thanksgiving, then I am forced to give in to the power of darkness. There is no beach in daylight for most of December and January. When the beach is available, it is usually too miserable to paddle.

Thanksgiving and Christmas are private holidays, hard to share with those you don't know. If we just had a saint's day or two, sometime in winter, then there would be an excuse for a fiesta. We could all smile at each other a bit as we paraded the heavy icons through the drizzle and choked on the sweet smell of incense. *That* would be something we could all agree on.

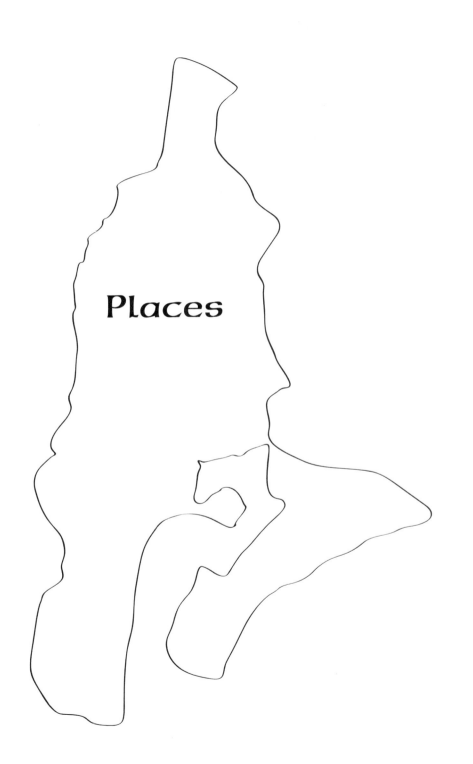

*I cannot come nearer to God and Heaven
Than I live to Walden even
I am its stony shore
And the breeze that passes o'er*

Thoreau

Places

When you come to Vashon to paddle with me, or even if you already live here, you need to know where to launch and maybe where to recover. You might like to get a drink or maybe use the restroom.

So I've put this little guide together for you, and that way you will never feel lost. These are the public places on Vashon where you and I and all our kayaking friends can put our boats in the water, and where we can get them out again.

We have to be careful, though. The tides, the currents and the weather all bear watching. This morning's placid lake is this afternoon's dangerous surf. This morning's beach will be under four feet of wave-driven water later.

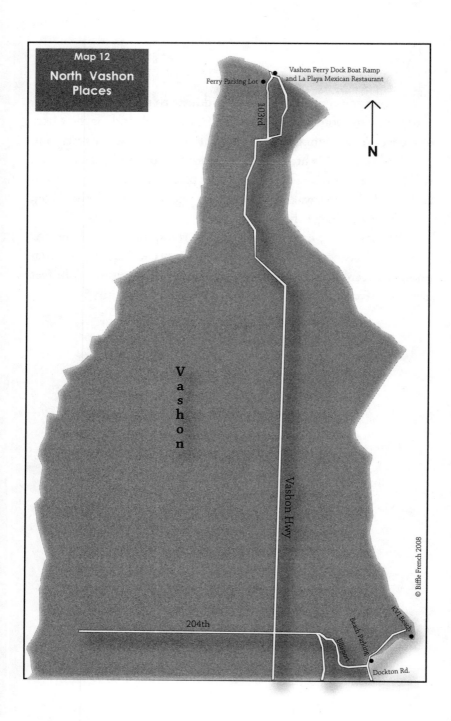

Vashon Ferry Dock

There is a public boat ramp at the Vashon Ferry Dock that can be used to launch and recover. It is not the best place on Vashon for several reasons, but it is public so you *can* use it if you want to and if you have enough experience to get past some of the difficulties.

There are some good things about this location. It has public restrooms (not just a Port-a-Potty) at the ferry terminal. La Playa, a popular Mexican restaurant, is located right on the dock, which makes it especially appealing if you are going to recover there. Get your boat out, chow down on Mexican food and have a beer or an iced tea. Nothing better than that after a long paddle.

There is also an espresso kiosk located just across the ferry dock from the boat ramp, but it is just open weekday mornings. And there is parking—sometimes.

From Vashon Highway, take 103rd Ave SW which leads to the ferry parking area and passenger pickup (such as it is). At the stop sign you will be looking directly at the Mexican Restaurant parking lot straight ahead. If ferry traffic is moving you have to wait. They have the right of way, and they will not be looking at you.

DON'T drive down Vashon Highway thinking that is more direct. You will be stuck in the ferry line, which stops for up to an hour sometimes. If you do get in the ferry line by mistake DO NOT cross the yellow line and risk a head-on with the ferry traffic coming up the hill. They will be racing each other to the bottleneck and they will not be looking for some suicidal tourist on the wrong side of the road. If the sheriff sees you do that you might get arrested. At the very least you will get an ass chewing, a very public Breathalyzer and a $400 ticket.

If you do find yourself stuck in the ferry line and there is no oncoming traffic, make a safe, legal U-turn, go back up the hill and look for 103rd Ave SW.

Once in the restaurant parking lot, look to your left and you will see the small boat ramp at the corner just next to the ferry dock.

The boat ramp is located at the northwest end of the Mexican restaurant parking lot and runs down parallel to the ferry dock.. The ramp is public, but getting there is a hassle since you have to cut across the ferry line and drive through the restaurant parking lot. Also, you can not park there. The parking lot is for restaurant patrons only. You will have to unload and park elsewhere.

The only parking is back up 103rd Ave SW at the large (and usually completely full) ferry parking area you passed on the way down. If the lot is full you can use street parking on one of the nearby streets. Weekends are usually easier, since a large number of weekday island commuters use the ferry parking lot to leave their cars while they walk onto boats or board buses for Seattle. The Seattle-bound buses ride the boats and you can board them at Vashon or at Fauntleroy when the boat docks there.

The boat ramp is a narrow concrete structure just wide enough for a boat trailer, which means that a kayak can not easily be launched in the normal manner parallel to the water, but may need to be put in using the 90° method. However, that's tough, too, because the ramp is quite steep, maybe 10° or so, which would cause your bow to be in maybe 18" of water while the stern is still on the rough concrete. All in all, it's a difficult launching or recovery situation when the tide is above the bottom of the ramp.

At about sea level 8' or slightly less, the bottom of the ramp is out of the water. At that point it's easier to launch or recover because you can just land on the rocky beach.

There is another option if the tide is too high, which is not recommended, but is better than smashing up your boat. You *could* recover (not launch) from the private beach on the west side of the ferry dock and sneak out their gate before anyone notices. It's private property and they don't want you there, but if you can't land at the boat ramp you may have no other choice. I'm not advocating that you do this, just suggesting it as a possible life-saving approach if the situation becomes otherwise hopeless.

Vashon Ferry Dock

I usually don't like to launch from this location because of the hassles. I *do* sometimes recover from there for three reasons. First, there is bus service from there to much of the island, which means you can spot your car there and take the bus home to start your paddle. That's important to me, since I don't always have someone available to give me rides.

Second, since this location is at the north end of the island, it is downhill from everything on the west side. Starting here would be much more difficult for those trips, since you would be pulling against a strong current the whole way.

And finally, there is some pretty good Mexican food there, so it's a great place to wind up at lunchtime or dinnertime.

Tramp Harbor

Tramp Harbor is a large indentation in the east side of Vashon island extending about a mile from about the middle of Maury Island to the KVI beach. I might call it a "bay" rather than a "harbor," since it is not really very protected, but then I did not name it.

This area of the island is very different from the steep cliffs that characterize much of the rest of the shoreline. If you look at a navigation chart you can see that the one-fathom contour is maybe 500 feet from the high tide mark. That is a very gradual decline. Because of the shape of the island here, silt and sand have collected over eons and much of the beach is quite soft. There is a nice view across the East Passage from much of the harbor and you can see the new control tower at SeaTac from this location, as well as Normandy Park and Des Moines.

Tramp Harbor has three locations where kayakers can launch: the fishing pier on Dockton Road, the parking lot at the three-way intersection of Dockton, Ellisport and Chautauqua Beach roads, and KVI Beach. All are OK, but none is perfect.

Driving north on Dockton Road from Portage, there is a new fishing pier with steps to the beach that can be used as a launch area for kayaks. There is a small parking lot right by the steps that can hold four or five cars, and a long fishing pier that is a fun attraction all by itself. There is a handy Port-a-Potty there. Vehicle traffic is rather heavy in this area by Vashon standards, so you need to take care to avoid getting hit, as the parking spots are much too close to the busy road for safety.

There are two sets of steps to the beach. The north steps lead down to a difficult area with large stones and a small, tricky launch area too near the pier pilings for comfort. The south steps lead to a beautiful gravel beach paved with pea-sized stones that looks like it was made for Kayak launching. King County in their august wisdom has made parking illegal near the south steps even though there is plenty of room to do it. So there is really no safe, legal way for a kayaker to unload a kayak and put it on the beach here. There are some other things about this launch site that I don't like, which make it my least favorite.

First, legal parking is head in only, which means that a kayak has to be unloaded right into the traffic. The illegal parking south steps lead to an easily-accessible sloping beach that is great for launching with one important caveat: it is under four feet of water at high tide. Sea level must drop below about eight feet in order for you to launch or recover from this location, so make sure you consult the tide charts carefully before you make the decision to use this beach. If you launch into a rising tide, you may not be able to get back.

When the tide is in you will be confronted with deep water sloshing constantly against a concrete bulkhead, barnacle-covered pilings and concrete steps, which may be impossible to get to. Exiting the boat under these conditions can be quite dangerous, especially if there is any surf at all. Personally, I would never risk it.

The roadside parking area at the three-way-intersection of Dockton, Ellisport and Chautauqua definitely offers the best vehicle access. Green algae covers the beach here, indicating a supply of fresh water from a spring or creek. There is plenty of parking with a lot more room for unloading a boat. There are no restroom facilities, but the Port-a-Potty at the fishing pier is only a couple hundred yards away. At low tide there is a bit of a hike across the muddy, algae-covered beach to the water. I like this location best because of the easy parking, in spite of the lack of a rocky beach. It is the only one I ever use.

The third location is the KVI beach. This popular beach belongs to radio station KVI, and is the site of their transmission tower. It is a beautiful spot and could be great for launching. The big problem is that parking is quite difficult. Narrow, winding 204th street offers the only access. This little lane was never intended for street parking, and there is only a little to be had. The closest parking spots give a relatively easy, short portage, but if you can't park close you will be in for a struggle. This is my second favorite of the three locations.

All that said, however, with a little planning, and under the right conditions, once you are in the water Tramp Harbor can be a great place to kayak.

When the tide is between say, six and eight feet, you are just above the sandy or muddy beach and can stay that way over a very large area since the slope is so gradual. Kayaking above a shallow beach is like flying low. If the water is clear you can see everything on the bottom and everything in the water. Dogfish, flounder, jellyfish, snails – they are all there like in an aquarium, but they are free. And so are you. It's kind of like snorkeling on top.

After launching at Tramp Harbor you can just stay in the local area, which is great for beginners, especially if you just play in the shallows. Or you can easily get as far into deep water as you like. Less than one mile northeast of the shallows, a steep gorge drops to nearly eight hundred feet. Point Robinson with stony beach and lighthouse is about three and a half miles southeast. Vashon ferry dock with traffic, beer and Mexican food is about seven miles north.

Or, if you are really adventurous, an expert paddler and have a well-thought-out support system you can paddle due east about six miles across open water, strong currents and the heavily-traveled Puget Sound Traffic Lane to Des Moines Beach Park. Out and back for that trip is about three hours of steady paddling with no wind or current for a strong paddler, so know your capabilities and understand the conditions before you tackle it. A kayaker is completely out of sight at a distance of well under a mile. If anything goes wrong, no one on shore will know.

Point Defiance, Owen Beach, Ruston

Directly south across Dalco Pass from Tahlequah there is a large park on what used to be a military reservation. It's name, "Point Defiance" conjures up visions of WW II gun emplacements manned by nervous soldiers nightly expecting a dawn Japanese invasion. It might have happened that way, but it didn't. No military facilities were ever built there.

Teddy Roosevelt, the great creator of parks, preserver of natural beauty, and single-handed creator of the nation of Panama out of a piece of land that Columbia no longer needed, gave the reservation to the City of Tacoma in 1905. He did this while the Japanese were still whipping up on China, Russia and Korea. No one expected "the Japs" to try to run the Narrows in gunboats, and they never did. The Japanese invasion of Washington petered out right after they opened a sushi restaurant in Tacoma.

Point Defiance never defied anybody. It has always been there just for fun, and it still is.

The Boathouse at Point Defiance was a tradition for years, and the building, now refurbished, is currently occupied by Anthony's. The Anthony's chain is known for reliable, quality seafood and great service at waterside locations throughout Puget Sound and the Point Defiance Anthony's is no exception. It is located just a couple hundred feet from the Point Defiance end of the Point Defiance/Tahlequah Ferry.

It's a lot cheaper to walk on the ferry than to take a vehicle, and walk-ons never have to wait. When the boat is full, cars are stuck in line, while walk-ons always board. For that reason, locals often walk onto the ferry for a dinner at Anthony's, as my wife and I did one Sunday in summer a few years ago.

We dined early, since we both had planes to catch the next morning, which for us means a cruel 3 o'clock wake up. So by seven o'clock Sunday night we were ready to go home, relax a bit and try to sleep early. We strolled across the short sidewalk from Anthony's to the ferry

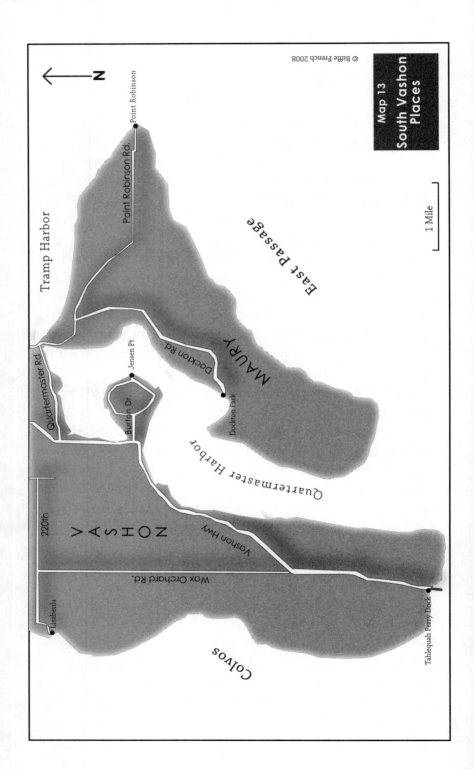

terminal, presented our tickets and heard the bad news.

"Ferry's not running. The slip is busted on the Vashon side. Hydraulic fluid is leaking and we have a containment crew out there now. We may be down all night."

"Eek."

I am nothing if not flexible, so I formulate a winning plan. I will get one of the boaters who are taking their boats out at the boat ramp to make just one more trip (it's just over a mile) and I will pay them handsomely for the effort.

"How about fifty bucks for a ride to Vashon? It's just right over there."

"Whut?"

"The ferry broke and we don't have our car. Could you give us a ride across to Vashon?"

The man looked trapped, confused. I noticed that the entire floor space of his 12-foot aluminum boat was covered with a layer of beer cans. Could they all be from today?

"Whut?"

"Never mind, I see you are busy. I'll ask someone else."

But no one else wanted to take us, either. When people are ready to haul out, nothing can reverse that decision, not even fifty bucks. Eventually, we found a ride to Southworth, walked on to the Issaquah, and called a friend on our cell. We got about four hours sleep that night and never walked on the Rhody again for years. The ferries are our life. Without them, all is chaos.

The park at Point Defiance has been so for over 100 years now, and it has long been the prize of Tacoma. There are woods, a five-mile drive, a long beach, boat rentals, a Rose Garden and lovely pavilions. There is a wonderful aquarium and a nice zoo. The Taste of Tacoma is held there on the weekend before the 4th of July. I never go there then, since I am the sort of person who enjoys calm, solitary pleasures like kayaking alone and abhors a crowd. But you should, if you like that sort of thing.

PLACES

There is a parking lot at the beach at Point Defiance, in an area called Owen Beach. It is a reliable and relatively easy place to launch from. There is usually plenty of parking there, although the lot is steep and you may do better to unload on the flat at the bottom, such as it is. From the parking lot to the beach is a short carry of maybe 100 yards. You will never have this part of the beach to yourself, since it is popular with locals year round. If there were still truant officers, they would have easy pickings there.

Any of the trips from Tahlequah can also be done from Owen Beach, and that especially applies to the roundabouts. If you live in Tacoma and want to paddle south Vashon, then launching from Owen is a great way to manage it without having to hassle with the ferry. There is a length charge, so carrying your kayak on the Rhody is probably going to cost the same regardless of whether you take your truck.

If you do decide to launch from Owen Beach be sure you have a plan for dealing with the Narrows current. It is all quite placid right there at the launch, but as soon as you get fifty feet west of the Point itself, you are in the Narrows current, which during powerful tides may run much faster than you can paddle. If the tide is ebbing and the current is going north, so will you. If it is flooding, and the current is going south, a careless kayaker could find him or herself looking up at the bottom of the Narrows Bridge and wondering how to avoid big whirlpools and the bridge supports. Caveat kayaker.

Dockton

Dockton Park is a good, sheltered location with plenty of facilities including restrooms, plenty of flat parking, picnic tables and even showers. There are also fire pits and even a little playground for those who enjoy that sort of thing.

Kayakers will find a nice grassy area for staging and a boat dock with a long floating walkway in case you want to try your low dock entry. Except for the marinas, which are private, this is the only place on Vashon where you can get into or out of a kayak without using a beach entry. If you know how enter this way, you can stay completely dry, head to toe, for the whole trip.

The beach at Dockton leaves something to be desired, since it is mostly pretty muddy. I almost lost a sneaker there once, while trying to get out of my boat. It stuck fast in the deep mud and refused to come free. If you can use the dock safely, then that is a more pleasant way to get in and out of your boat.

Dockton is a mile or so from Jensen Point, so for short paddles starting there gives you different experiences than starting at Jensen. The Dockton area itself is really interesting, both on land and near the water. The steep hills above the park have some beautiful houses with views of Quartermaster. There is an odd collection of boats moored in the area, including some derelicts that appear to be residences and have seen better days.

If you paddle to the north, you will get back to the Burton Peninsula and Jensen Point. If I were going to do that, I'd rather start at Jensen, since the inner harbor is more accessible from there. But if you paddle to the south, it's a different story.

South of Dockton and around Dockton Point you enter outer Quartermaster Harbor. If you are a beginner, then this is a step towards open water paddling that allows you to rather quickly retreat in case you get tired, need to use the restroom or can't handle the conditions.

Most of the time conditions in Quartermaster are the most benign anywhere, but sometimes when the wind is strong, there is enough fetch to raise some waves that may be too much for many kayakers. The wind most commonly blows from the south, and a strong south wind blowing across Commencement Bay and up the narrow corridor of outer Quartermaster Harbor can deliver some real surprises.

I have left home for an easy paddle in Quartermaster more than once and found myself nearly unable to return, confronted with winds so strong that I could not make headway. Sometimes I have to hug the shoreline hoping that the friction from the bluffs will slow the wind just enough to let me get past Neil Point. Once out of the harbor and paddling west, the wind is not so strong and it is possible to proceed more easily. There was one occasion when I chose to pick my way through the boulder field at Neil Point rather than try to get far enough south to safely clear the Point Rock. I just didn't see how I could physically manage to paddle that far into the teeth of the gale.

So, yes. Quartermaster, like any other wet place can be treacherous. If you're not a skilled and practiced paddler beware of the winds, since they can be magnified greatly in the outer harbor. When you are coming from Dockton Park, look at the surface of the water before you round Dockton Point. If the water west of the point is rougher than the water east of it, be prepared for a shock.

When it's not windy, though, and most of the time it's not, there are some beautiful things to see in outer Quartermaster. Two paddles that I like are the loop around the whole inner harbor, which is whatever distance you choose and the Piner Point out-and-back, which is about two miles round trip.

There are a few small communities—neighborhoods really—on Quartermaster beaches, but much of the shoreline is unpopulated. All the beaches are private property, but there is no one to say "no" in many places and there are no "No Trespassing" signs. I admit to stopping for a rest or a picnic now and then.

Piner Point is protected by the Vashon Land Trust, so it is private property as well, but they do allow you to stop there for a bit and enjoy the beautiful spot. Landing there is usually easy unless there is surf.

Point Robinson

Point Robinson Park is my second-favorite launching site on Vashon Island. I like Jensen Point just a bit more because it is much more sheltered from wind and surf, but Point Robinson runs a very close second.

This is another great Vashon park, and it has a lot of charms. There is a long, pebble-covered beach that is great for a stroll, and has nice views to the east and north. And then, of course, there is the beautiful lighthouse, which is a real treasure.

The Coast Guard established a station at Point Robinson in 1885 that had some kind of light associated with it as early as 1887. The station also had rescue boats, and according to one of the volunteers who manage the site today, the four-wheeled cart next to the tower was used to quickly launch the big rowboats in emergencies by rolling them down rails into the water.

I try to imagine those tough young men, with their handlebar moustaches and striped wool clothing, just awakened, sleep still in their eyes, agilely climbing into one of those big, open rowboats and rolling in it down the clattering steel rails into the pounding surf. Each one pulled on the oars with all his might, knowing that they had just minutes to rescue their charges from drowning. Sometimes they returned with their corpses. Sometimes they did not return at all.

All that remains today is the cart and the beautiful light, which wasn't built until 1915, thirty years after the first station. Whenever I go there I think about how different their lives were from ours. They never expected things to be instant, perfect and free like so many brainwashed Americans do now, watching CNN, clucking at any imperfection and expecting their nanny government to solve every problem for them.

These heroes fought the frigid surf, saved the living and claimed the dead. They were mighty, but they suffered miserably and sometimes they died. They knew a true life, face to face with nature.

For us, it's a park now, a public place we ride to in our warm, dry cars, see the water and sit on the beach. The park is open from dawn to dusk and there is usually enough parking. Most people don't stay too long, so the parking spots get recycled. The Coast Guard sails in Zodiacs these days.

There are two refurbished keeper's houses at the park that are rented to visitors. I think it would be great fun to stay there, since the site is so beautiful. For a kayaker it would be perfect, since both houses are right on the beach.

To get to Point Robinson from downtown, go south on Vashon Highway and turn left on SW Ellisport Rd. which becomes Dockton Rd SW. Bear left on SW Point Robinson Rd. at the Y and follow it to the end. Turn right to enter the park.

The park road is narrow and steep so watch for other traffic, especially pedestrians and bicycles. At the bottom of the road there is a flat parking area with space for maybe ten cars. I try to park by the Port-a-Potties, since that is the easiest unload zone and gives the best access to the beach.

Scout the short, level path to the beach before unloading so you don't stumble around foolishly carrying a heavy kayak and looking for a break in the grass and logs. The path just beside the caretaker's fence is the one you want and it takes you to a good launch site.

From Point Robinson you can travel south to Piner Point or north to Tramp Harbor. These are both exposed routes, but if you stay near shore you are out of the way of the giant container ships coming up and down the Puget Sound Traffic Lane. You will not be protected against wind, power boats, ship wakes or tidal currents, though, so make sure you know what the conditions are before you get too far away from the launch.

Places

Lisabeula

To get to Lisabeula Park, take SW 220th Street west all the way to the end, then turn left onto Lisabeula Road. This is a steep, winding one-lane road traveled by bicyclists as well as cars, so please drive slowly. The park is open dawn to dusk. It used to be open all the time, but local teens were "having too much fun" there, so the decision was made to close it at night. Now the beer-bottle patrol does not have to work as hard. But don't plan to leave your car there after dark.

The road runs beside a deep ravine that is forested with alder trees and covered with ferns. It is one of those places on the island that still give you the brief, delicious feeling of the forest primeval. You expect to see parrots, and will be disappointed in that, but you may see herons and eagles, osprey and terns. There may be seals or sometimes sea lions in the water, and possibly river otters if you are early enough.

The little road ends in a large flat area with parking for several cars. There is a Port-a-Potty as well as trash and recycling containers. A few picnic tables are placed facing the beach to maximize the diner's views. This is my favorite park on Vashon. I think anyone who likes to be near the water will enjoy this park for it's own sake, regardless of whether they come with a kayak strapped to their truck or not.

This is a great location to launch from for a long trip or just to kayak in the local area. The beach is sandy or muddy in some places and covered with pebbles or stones in others, so you should scout the best location if you have a preference. I have recovered to Lisabeula and found myself walking a long way across mud, when a better scouting job beforehand would have had me land closer and on firm beach.

The beach is never steep, though, and much of it is usable. The only obvious hazard is a buried cable, which I think is probably deep enough not to cause a problem for kayakers, although I always stay well clear of that area. I've never seen the cable, only the sign. That ugly warning sign is a rare blight on an otherwise lovely location.

The current always runs north from Lisabeula—during the ebb

and during the flood. If you are just paddling locally, I recommend starting out to the south so you can come back "downhill." A nice local paddle is Lisabeula to Spring Beach Park and back, a round trip of about four miles.

Spring Beach Park is just south of the community of Spring Beach. You can recognize the Spring Beach neighborhood by a few old pilings that are in front of a beautiful beach front house with a sign that says "Miramar." That house is on a street with other houses that ends at a concrete bulkhead with a boat ramp. It is hard to miss. The park itself is a hundred acres or so of forested land with a good sandy beach. There are no facilities of any kind, and steep bluffs will keep you on the beach. That's perfectly OK, though since this beach is one of the best anywhere and it's always great for a stroll, a picnic or just a rest.

If you continue south of Spring Beach Park, especially near the shore, you will possibly be caught in the southbound eddy, which can be quite powerful as you approach Dalco Point. During a strong ebb you may not be able to return the way you came, since there can be a five-knot or stronger current in that area swirling to the south. You will not be able to overcome that, and it will take you places you may not want to go, including into wicked tide rips that are "experts only" terrain.

To return to Lisabeula from Spring Beach Park, paddle northwest out to the center of the Colvos and look for the reliable northbound current. Most of the time you will be able to coast back with very little effort.

Places

Tahlequah

At the south end of Vashon a small stream called the Tahlequah empties into the Puget Sound. There is a long steep-sided ravine that corrals the little flow, which starts around 280th Street, just above Spring Beach. Since Vashon was shaped by glacial and seismic forces, and since the amount of water is tiny, it seems unlikely that such a small rivulet created the wide chasm. More likely the water just found the gorge a convenient place to go. On the mainland, where hills are taller and canyons longer, the Tahlequah would be a dangerous place to be during a storm. I suppose it could be here, too, although there are houses built quite close to the stream bed and they have been there for quite a long time.

Just east of where the stream empties, the Tahlequah Ferry Dock stands. This dock replaced a terminus of the Mosquito fleet, whose ruin rots just beside it. There is no sign indicating public access to the beach, and in fact all the surrounding beaches are private. However, there is a trail on the west side of the ferry bridge that leads to the tidelands below the ferry slip. At mid tide it is possible to launch from there, although schlepping a kayak down the steep trail is easier with two people. The top part of the trial is a wide, flat moderately-steep old road with cracked asphalt pavement. Below that there is a sandy section that is not too difficult to manage. At the bottom of the sand there is a low bulkhead, about three feet high. That is the tricky part, and getting a kayak across that little barrier needs to be done carefully if you are going to avoid injury to yourself or your boat.

This is not a perfect location for kayakers, and if you want to try it, you are on your own. Make sure you scout the trail first to see that you can really do it. King County has said that they will improve access to the beach at the ferry terminal, but at the moment the situation could be better. Still, once you are at the bottom there is a flat rocky beach to launch from, and the area is protected from much of the wake surf that plagues Vashon beaches during the best part of kayak season. (Kayak season is all 12 months, of course. The best part is from February to November. Wake surf is mostly a problem on weekends from Memorial Day to Labor Day.)

The advantages of launching from Tahlequah Ferry are that it's public property with some available local parking, a reasonably-good beach, and access to some really good kayaking in the immediate vicinity. There is a Port-a-Potty on the ferry bridge in case you need some last minute adjustments prior to launch.

The main disadvantage of launching from Tahlequah Ferry, is that once the tide level gets above 8' or even less, depending on wave activity, you can not land again. There is no longer any beach, and you may be stuck for hours unable to get back. Don't let that happen to you. It is no fun to arrive at the take-out point tired, hungry and with a full bladder only to discover that you can not land. Check the tide charts carefully before launching from Tahlequah!!! Make sure you can get back!!!

Parking and unloading at Tahlequah Ferry are problematic, but not impossible. You will likely be towed if you park illegally on the south side of the street. You will definitely get into a shouting match or a fistfight if you try to unload or park on the bridge or in the ferry line. Violating ferry etiquette is a hanging offense on Vashon. However, you can unload on the south side of the street in the "No Parking" area just east of the electronic "Tahlequah" sign. Don't stay there more ten minutes or so. Once you have unloaded, park east of the ferry on the north side of the street or up the ramp in the parking lot across from the terminal. If you don't know east from north, you are not ready for this location. Go to Jensen Point, where it doesn't matter.

Tahlequah, as the surrounding area is known, is completely built up at the beach. There are a few houses north the road as well, but much of the surrounding area is unbuildable. From Neil Point on the East to Dalco Point on the West, there are private houses and private beaches everywhere. Access to the beach is difficult everywhere, since the area is mostly quite steep. In my case, for instance, I have to climb 60 vertical feet with kayak and gear, something that took me a while to master. I don't have to cross a bulkhead, but other than that, access is easier at the ferry dock.

Once in the water at Tahlequah, Owen Beach is just over a mile to the south, Point Defiance is about two miles to the southwest, Dalco Point is west about 3/4 mile and Neil Point is east just over a mile. Those are all interesting locations in their own right, and they are all gateways to a wider and more interesting world of kayaking.

Jensen Point

Of all the spots on Vashon Island, Jensen Point, located in Burton Acres Park, is the best and most reliable one for launching and landing a kayak. There is plenty of free parking almost any time (except for 4th of July, when the free fireworks draw the entire population of the island). There is a grassy lawn and tables for picnicking. There is a well-kept, and almost new, public restroom. Across the road there is a beautiful hiking trail that circles the entire center of the Burton Peninsula. The trail is flat enough for almost any ambulatory person to enjoy.

Then there are the kayaking facilities.

Jensen Point is home to Puget Sound Kayaks (206-463-YAKS). The large boathouse at Jensen contains their collection of single and double kayaks, paddles, and assorted auxiliary gear. The boathouse, which belongs to King County Parks, is also filled with racing sculls of various sizes used by local rowing teams.

These long sleek white fiberglass boats are fun just to look at. They remind me of the Grob sailplanes I used to fly at the Caddo Mills airport in Texas. Now *that's* a sport! Thermaling in one of those beauties in the boiling skies of Texas on a hot summer day was like being on a dynamite-powered elevator. I have many times been to eight thousand feet off a five hundred foot tow, climbing in a steep bank, so fast and so roughly that my passenger puked all over the cloth seat and occasionally down the back of my T-shirt. They were always surprised to see the wings flex violently with all the power of those explosive thermals. Some just couldn't contain their excitement.

Jensen Point has a great launching/recovery area for kayaks, power boats and racing sculls. Locals put in their trailered fishing craft or sailboats there, and it's relatively uncrowded, since mainlanders get no advantage from paying the hefty length charge to load their boats on the ferry just to launch free at Vashon. During a weekday, or even a Saturday morning during the summer, I have often felt downright lonely at this prime location.

The grassy lawn leads to a flat pebbled beach and the parking lot

takes trailers or kayaks to the gentle boat ramp. The sheltered location is proof against wake surf except for local traffic coming out of inner Quartermaster Harbor. This is the place for novices, and it is certainly one that experts will enjoy as well. I always feel a harmonious sense of perfection whenever I take myself down to Jensen. It is world class.

The adventurous can travel anywhere from Jensen, and they can rent kayaks there if they don't happen to be packing when the mood strikes them. Novices can paddle around in the safest environment available, staying close to the take out in case they get tired, scared, angry with each other or just had enough. It's three miles from the launch site to the mouth of Quartermaster harbor which promises plenty of kayaking without ever having to risk open water. The short trip to Dockton park, south across the harbor, is pleasant although landing a kayak there is not as easy, owing to the muddy bottom. The most protected area to the north is fun, with lots of nice houses and boats to look at. Circling inner Quartermaster harbor can be done in about an hour and that is plenty for a lot of folks, especially those who are just getting used to a kayak.

Anyone who kayaks on Vashon for the first time should definitely start out on Jensen point. Try the more interesting locations later, after you understand the local environment better. Jensen is definitely the place to start.

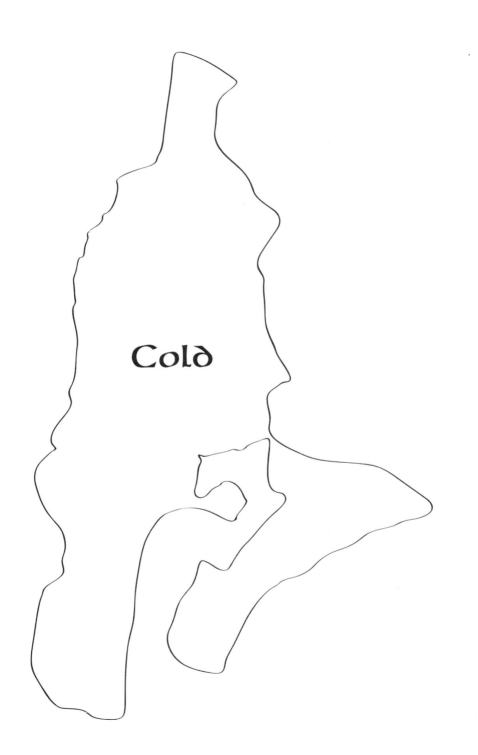

Good Judgment Comes from Experience. Experience comes from bad judgment.

General Lee

Cold Water Paddling

According to NOAA's "Coastal Water Temperature Guide," the water temperature for Seattle normally varies from a high of about 56° Fahrenheit in August to a low of 47° in January. They don't give figures for Vashon, but I suppose that's pretty close.

Call me a sissy, but when I lived in Texas, where it is really hot and miserable most of the time in summer, I usually waited until the water temp in my pool hit the high 80's before I felt a need to jump in. I don't need to tell you that 56° water is chilly, no matter how hot that August day is. In January, when the air temperature is 35°, the 47° water may not seem so bad at first, but it is.

A couple years ago one of the neighborhood dogs ran down a deer on our beach. The deer panicked and leapt into the water. It swam well out into the Dalco Pass, then swam back when the dog was gone. When it stepped up onto the beach, it collapsed and died. The very same thing happens to people.

Average life expectancy in 50° water is *one hour*, but that's just an average. Life expectancy increases as the water temperature increases, but around Vashon the water temperature is 50° or below most of the year, so figure on that. Swimming in cold water actually *decreases* your survival time, especially if your head is under that water. In many cases survival is just 30 minutes, and often swimmers who make a long swim to shore collapse and die in just a few minutes. If you fall out of your boat and can't self rescue or swim to shore within just a few minutes, you will not get to collect your Social Security check.

Very frequently, especially in summer, I see people kayaking here who do not take the conditions seriously. Most of them get away with it, as I have gotten away with so many things during my life, because most of them never fall in the water. But if you want to be around for the ride home, you need a plan that will get you out of the water quickly if you *do* fall in. If that plan is to swim for shore, you need to stay in close so you can really do that. It's easy to find yourself too far out to swim back. Concentrate on remaining within just a few yards of the beach.

If your plan is to self rescue, then you need to ask yourself whether you have practiced that recently. If you never practiced it at all, I guarantee you that you can not do it. There is some important element of it that you never knew or don't remember. Floating in that frigid water, like Leonardo in Titanic, things are not funny any longer. Your life is at stake here: take it seriously.

Neighbors tell of a case locally a few years back where two young men rented a double kayak for a trip around Owen Beach. Out in the middle, about a mile from shore, one of the guys needed to answer nature's call, and foolishly stood up to take care of that. His balance was bad and he dumped the two of them into the Sound. Now I suppose you can get back into a double if you know how and have the right equipment, but doubles are big and clumsy, and I don't know if I could do it, since I've never tried.

The guys tried to get back in for a while, but then after a bit they realized that they did not really know how, so they decided to swim for it. Being young guys and in good shape, they both made it to shore, but when they got up onto the beach one of them collapsed and died of hypothermia-induced heart attack right there. Once the damage is done, your body just fails. It's like running out of gas.

You can increase your exposure time by quite a lot with proper clothing. Shorts and a T-shirt have no value at protecting you, but if it's summer and you wear a dry suit, you will be miserable in a few minutes and have to take it off. If it's cool enough I wear a Polartec outfit made for river kayakers, which works pretty well at keeping you warm once you are back out of the water, but it isn't much help at all while you are in there. However, in summer, I am forced to go the shorts and a T-shirt route as well, since it is no good to overheat while you are paddling. In my case, though, I know I can get back in the boat in well under five minutes, and I know it because I practice it from time to time, so I figure I'm taking a pretty small chance.

I always try to know the risks I'm taking. When I owned a Citabria I used to do aerobatics without a parachute, figuring that parachutes were just one more thing to mess with and if the wings folded up I would not be able to get out anyway, due to the G forces and the failed structure crumpled all around me. One day I mishandled an aileron roll, found myself inverted, accelerating through red line, and was forced to revisit that analysis. In general, though, no one gets out of a broken airplane, parachute or no parachute, but people can self rescue in kayaks if they take the trouble to learn how.

Cold water will kill you pretty quickly, so respect it and have a plan to save your life if you go in. The only plan that will work is one you have practiced until you have it down pat.

Kayak self rescue is best taught by a qualified instructor. Tacoma Mountaineers offers a one-week school every year in spring to teach all manner of kayaking skills. If you have the time to do that, I highly recommend it. There is also a Kayak Symposium every spring that lasts two days at Owen Beach in Tacoma. Vashon Kayaks teaches rescue techniques, so if you live on Vashon or visit during the summer, that is a great way to learn to save your life. Lake Union has at least one organization that teaches kayaking, and there may be more. If none of these places is near where you live, look online for kayak instruction near you.

Of course, it is not just about saving *your* life. You may need to save someone else instead. Buddy rescues are also taught in these classes so you can get another person back in *their* boat. *Both* parties have to know the technique, since it is unlikely that you will teach a panicky paddler who is experiencing really cold water for the first time how to help you rescue them. If you go into the water with that person, then you will *both* likely die.

I won't bother to try to describe self-rescue techniques here, since I really don't think it's an appropriate skill to learn from a book. Find an instructor, take classes and then practice at least a couple times a year in a safe place close to shore.

If you want to understand the techniques better before getting instruction, then get Bill Seidman's book "The Essential Sea Kayaker" which gives a very good description of the basic approaches.

The two primary pieces of rescue gear you will need are a paddle float and a hand bailing pump. I like the SealLine paddle float sold by REI, which is easy to attach once you are in the water. Look for a bailing pump with a large exit port, since you want to get any water out of the boat quickly and a small exit port slows you down.

Learn to get out of cold water. Paddle again tomorrow.

Epílog

One generation abandons the enterprises of another like stranded vessels

                                                 Thoreau

Tomorrow

It makes me wistful to say it, but the Vashon we know today will be lost. The sand is running out of the glass and can not be put back in. It will differ by degree – a little here, a little there, until it becomes as different from the island we know today as today's is from the one Vancouver discovered in 1792. You can not hold back the tide, and you can not keep Vashon.

Just at the moment it is as wonderful a place as can be found on the planet. That very fact is what will alter it. Each person who sees it wants a chunk for himself, but by the getting of it, makes it entirely something else. And those are just the loving hands, others have different motives.

Lone Star, a Japanese company, wants to mine large sections of Maury Island for gravel. It is their land, it is their gravel and they have most of the permits they need. We have held them back for seven years at this point, but the property is worth $50,000,000 give or take a bit, and no person or corporation is ever going to walk away from that kind of money. Islanders can find funds to hire attorneys and lobby legislators, but getting the cash to buy out Lone Star and turn the gravel pit into a park seems unlikely. The few who are most affected would probably have to come up with the bulk of the money, and it would run to millions each. They just can't afford it, and no Mysterious Benefactor stands in the wings. Some look to the state, but that is fantasy because the state sees its interests aligned with the mine operator rather than a few pitiful supplicants standing in the way of progress. Gravel is needed for roads and runways, not parks on rural islands.

Mike Cohen, who purchased the Asarco property recently and is developing Point Ruston wants to put an amphitheater just barely a mile across the water from south Vashon and Maury Islands. Unbearably loud music would emanate from the site at volumes approaching the threshold of pain, and ruin peace and tranquility for anyone living within the high decibel impact area which includes Vashon, Maury,

Epilog

North Tacoma, Ruston, Brown Point and Gig Harbor.

There are many who support this plan and many who oppose it. Whatever happens with the amphitheater, the Point Ruston development sits in the middle of the largest undeveloped piece of waterfront inside any city limits in the United States. Now that the cleanup is "finished," something is going to be different over there. It will be dramatic, it will be soon and it will change the sleepy southern part of Vashon Island forever.

An islander who ran a horse farm on the island was killed in a car crash along with his wife a few years back, and they left their holdings to the LDS church. The church wants to turn the property into a Mormon retreat of some type, and they want to be able to bring hundreds of young people to spend a week there each summer, living in a small city that they would construct. What is now a quiet ex-horse farm would become a buzzing hive of activity with many large new buildings, a giant water tower and constant traffic passing through rural neighborhoods.

Some of the local community have an objection to that plan on several grounds, but the one that concerns people most is their use of water. They want to take enough water to support that large community by pumping from the aquifer water that legally belongs to others. And they want to dump several thousand gallons a day back into the aquifer at a single point without any treatment other than a large septic system. All these things give us great pause and have caused many sleepless nights here on the south end of Vashon.

The Church has threatened to parcel out their land in two-acre plots if their plans can not be approved. Of course they would be well within their rights to do that, so we may soon see a housing development where today there is farmland.

Tom Stewart, scion of the island and its largest landowner, has decided that he will not let the State of Washington confiscate his estate upon his demise, as they would do under current law, so he has moved to Arizona, which has more favorable estate arrangements. He has put his Vashon property up for sale. It is now a cattle ranching operation and an abattoir. Some of it was a run-down apple orchard until just a few years ago. What will that big, central piece of grassy cow pasture become now?

The Land Trust, for instance, probably does not have the money to buy such a large parcel of land, and I wonder where they can ever get it. Inheritance laws aimed at redistributing wealth inexorably slice the planet into smaller pieces, and so the unfenced open tracts disappear. The rich man's once-big ranch becomes tiny ranchettes for everyman.

There are those who want desperately to preserve the natural heritage of the island. Ironically, *this* island, the one we know today, was formed only after strawberry farming in the clearcut was given up as uneconomic in the mid 20th century. It is not at all like the primeval forest known by the Indians of Vancouver's time. Still, it is a great improvement over a soulless grid of tract homes, a few of which already exist here.

It is the ferries whose very inconveniences and inadequacies protect us from the developments that have reshaped Maury Island. If the fanciful bridges were ever to really be constructed, the Vashon of today would be dust in an instant. When a developer wants to turn a Tacoma slag heap into San Diego, it is not unrealistic, but when that same person turns his attention to this island, he faces the realities and limitations imposed by water transportation. There really is no way to make big developments work here as things currently stand.

Larger ferries could be built, but who would pay for them? Where would they dock? What roads would carry the traffic? If Vashon were Dubai where money flows from fountains while water is more valuable than gold, it might be possible. Someday anything might happen, but not yet.

Are *all* the changes that will come to Vashon bad? I don't think so. People look for a firm rock to stand on, but there is none, nor has there ever been. I wish the falling leaves would stay a bit longer, but, if I look closely, I can already see the buds that will flower in the spring. All

Epilog

living things change constantly, and our beloved Vashon is very much alive. It will become what its *new* caretakers wish it to be for the days it is in *their* charge.

There is one thing that will not change—the Waters of Vashon. The Colvos will always flow on as it does now, with it's regular currents that can deliver the paddler almost effortlessly from Point Defiance to the Vashon Ferry. Mount Dalco will still beget exciting tide rips that can sometimes give the sea kayaker thrills normally reserved for the river riders. And all around this beautiful island there will be always be cold, deep, salt water, murky or clear, blue or gray, filled every day with all manner of wonderful living things—seal, crab, orca, gray whales, jellyfish, octopus, salmon and thousands of others, from the microscopic to the enormous, so many that most of them only have Latin names and more are yet to be discovered.

That will all be here for you and for me and for our grandchildren and their grandchildren, as long as the earth is round. No one can take the Waters of Vashon away from us – we will always have them. We kayakers will always have this little island paradise, the best place on earth for a paddler.

Bibliography

Frank Bergon ed., *Journals of Lewis and Clark,* Penguin Nature Classics, 1989

Richard W. Blumenthal, *Early Exploration of Inland Washington Waters,* McFarland & Co Inc., North Carolina, USA, 2004

Richard W. Blumenthal, *With Vancouver in Inland Washington Waters: Journals of 12 Crewmen, April-June 1792,* McFarland & Co Inc., North Carolina, USA, 2007

H.W. Brands, *Andrew Jackson,* Anchor, USA, 2006

H.W. Brands, *The Age of Gold,* Anchor, USA, 2003

H.W. Brands, *Lone Star Nation,* Anchor, USA, 2005

Jorge Luis Borges, *Selected Poems,* Edited by Alexander Coleman, Penguin Press 1999

Vincent J. Cronin, *Catherine, Empress of all the Russias,* Harvill, London, 1978

Joseph J. Ellis, *His Excellency,* Alfred A. Knopf, USA, 2004

Ralph Waldo Emerson, *Nature,* 1836

James Gleick, *Chaos,* Penguin Books, New York, NY, USA, 1987

Thomas J. Glover, *Pocket Ref,* Sequoia Publishing 1995

Eugene N. Kozloff, *Seashore Life of the Northern Pacific Coast,* University of Washington Press, Seattle, WA, 1993

NOAA, *Coast Survey Chart Number 18474,* Shilshole Bay to Commencement Bay

Dallas Murphy, *Rounding the Horn,* Basic Books, New York, NY, USA, 2004

Octavio Paz, *Labyrinth of Solitude,* Grove Press, 1961

Antonio Pigafetta, *Viaggio Inorno al Mundo,* (Around the World with Magellan) 1522

George H. Reid, *Primer of Towing,* Cornell Maritime Press, Centreville, MD, USA, 2004

E.V. Rieu, Translator, Revised translation by D.C.H. Rieu, Homer, *The Odyssey,* Penguin Literature, 1991

Robert H. Ruby, *Indians of the Pacific Northwest,* University of Oklahoma Press, 1981

John Paul Sartre, *No Exit,* (Play) 1944

David Seidman, *The Essential Sea Kayaker,* Ragged Mountain Press, Camden, ME, USA, 1992

Smithsonian Institute, Eskimo diorama

Donald and Lillian Stokes, *Stokes Guide to Birds,* Little, Brown and Co., 1996

Richard M. Strickland, *The Fertile Fjord – Plankton in the Puget*

Sound, Puget Sound Books, 1983

Ed Swan, *The Birds of Vashon Island,* Vashon, Washington, The Swan Company, 2005

Henry David Thoreau, *Walden,* 1854

Randel Washburne, *Kayaking Puget Sound the San Juans and Gulf Islands,* Seattle, WA USA, The Mountaineers., 1999

U.S. Marine Corps, *Warfighting – The U.S. Marine Corps Book of Strategy,* Doubleday Currency, 1994

United States Coast Guard, *Rules of the Road*

WEBSITES

Aircraft Owners and Pilots Association (AOPA) website, *G-36 Bonanza,* Online at: http://www.aopa.org/pilot/features/2006/feat0610.html

NOAA, *Coastal Water Temperature Guide,* Online at: http://www.nodc.noaa.gov/dsdt/cwtg/npac.html

http://www.weather.com/weather/climatology/monthly/USWA0395 (Online table showing average monthly rainfall amounts for various areas of the country. Supplied by the Weather Channel)

http://www.mobilegeographics.com:81/calendar/year/6314.html (Online tide calendar showing tides for Neil Point as well as sunrise, sunset and moon phases)

U.S. Geological Survey, *Mount Rainier Volcano Lahar Warning Sys-*

tem, Online at http://volcanoes.usgs.gov/About/Highlights/RainierPilot/Pilot_highlight.html

Wikipedia, various articles including "Tides", "Algae", "Jellyfish", "Starfish", "George Vancouver", "Hull Speed", and others used for general information and source recommendations.

Washington State Ferry website, http://www.wsdot.wa.gov/ferries/.

Comarado, this is no book
Who touches this touches a man

Whitman

As a young man Biffle French tried, then abandoned, studies in drama, journalism, music, political science and business. He finally completed degrees in math, linguistics and computer science. He has been a salesman, dishwasher, itinerant musician, septic tank digger, math teacher, Army soldier, hamburger cook, union laborer, scab laborer, bricklayer's helper, Air Force pilot, computer programmer, Director of Engineering and information technology architect. He has lived and worked in many parts of the United States as well as England, Canada, México and Panamá. These days he paddles his lime-green NC-17 around Vashon Island, makes art from wood, reads history and philosophy and writes and publishes books. This is one of several current book projects.

Want More Copies?

If you would like to purchase more copies of this book you can easily buy them online at www.VashonKayakBook.com.

You can also mail orders to us at:

**Lao Mei Publications
P.O. Box 13403
Burton, WA 98013
USA**

If you prefer to mail a check, or send your credit card information through the mail, then please copy & mail the form below (please print):

Name: _____

Street address or P.O. Box: _____

Apartment Number: _____

Other Designation: _____

City: _____

State or Province: _____

Country: _____

Zip or Postal Code: _____

Credit Card Type (Visa/MC/Amex): _____

Credit Card Number: _____

Email address: _____

Phone Number: _____

We charge $4.00 shipping for the first book. Additional books are at $2.00 each (guaranteed for 2008). Shipping outside the U.S. is charged at $9.00 USD for the first book and $5.00 USD for each additional book. We charge applicable sales tax on all orders in WA.

Whether you order online (secure) or via regular mail we will never divulge your personal information to anyone except as required for credit card approval. We will not save your information either, so it will be removed from our system once your transaction has been completed. We do need some way to contact you in case of problems, so please provide either your phone number or email address.

If you are unsatisfied with your book you may return it properly packaged and in brand-new condition for a full refund. If your book is damaged in transit, you may return it for a replacement.